MONEY SECRETS AT THE RACETRACK

MONEY
SECRETS
AT THE RACETRACK

Barry Meadow

Published by
TR PUBLISHING
4227 High Grove Rd.
Templeton, CA 93465

(800) 378-2211
www.trpublishing.com

Special thanks to two gentlemen who combine knowledge of their subjects with the sincere desire to help others—Dick Mitchell (whose computer expertise always seemed handiest just when I needed it most) and Jim Quinn (who has thought longer and harder about handicapping than almost anyone else).

Library of Congress Catalog Card Number: 87-51583

ISBN 0-945322-02-X

Printed in the United States of America

TABLE OF CONTENTS

INTRODUCTION

Money Secrets at the Racetrack is a different kind of book about betting at the races.

There's no handicapping method or selection system in this book. It doesn't tell you how to pick winners.

It does tell you *how to make money.*

There are dozens of books that will explain handicapping to you. This volume makes no attempt to compete with these efforts.

There are fewer books that discuss money management. Most of what has been written about the subject has either (a) been wrong or (b) required an advanced mathematics degree to understand. I hope you'll find that this book falls into neither category.

The secret of making money at the racetrack—whether you're playing thoroughbreds, harness horses, quarterhorses, or greyhounds—is to exploit errors in the crowd's line.

The public loses the amount of the state-track takeout and breakage. Though this varies from state to state, and from one type of racing to another, the takeout tornado will sweep up roughly 20% of all money bet. Random betting is a 20% loser. However, because fans overbet longshots and underbet favorites, playing only the crowd's first choice—the betting favorite—will yield a smaller loss, around 12%. Still, a loss is a loss

—and we're not going to the track to donate. *You* can be a winner.

To win, you must understand your game well enough to make an accurate line for your contenders. If you can—and you follow our strategies —you'll win.

Racetrack betting is unlike those games with fixed percentages against you. Playing the pass line in craps, for instance, yields a disadvantage of 1.4%. While it is possible to lower your total disadvantage (by, for instance, taking triple odds at a casino that offers such a play), it is impossible to reduce the 1.4% disadvantage on pass-line bets. That's why there is no such animal as a professional craps player.

The racetrack, though it offers an overall 20% disadvantage, is actually a much better game than craps—because, if you're sharp enough to beat your competition, you have an edge. Let's say that you determine that a certain horse has a 35% chance to win its race, but its odds are 5-2. Every time you bet in this situation, you have an edge. For each $200 you bet, you'll receive, on average, $245 (35 wins × $7 mutuel).

The key to winning at racetrack betting is to *find these overlays, and then bet them correctly.* Underbet and your bankroll doesn't grow as fast as it should. Overbet and you can easily go bankrupt, even if you play with an advantage. All our bet charts in **Money Secrets at the Racetrack** have been scaled towards the conservative side—but as you win, you can increase your stakes.

I've tried to keep the mathematical explanations to a minimum. They're included only to explain how our strategies were developed. You won't need a fancy computer with expensive software to use any of them. Just attach our charts and a set of blank sheets (more about these later) to a clipboard, carry a $5 pocket calculator, and you're set.

While handicapping techniques change nearly from day to day (a track bias might overwhelm all other factors for a week, for instance), money management skills never vary. Once you understand the principles in this book, you'll never have to relearn them, or alter them if you switch from one sport to another.

Throughout this book, to avoid having to say "thoroughbred, standardbred, quarterhorse, and dog," we'll often just say "horse." Exotic bets will be called by the same names throughout—quinella, exacta, trifecta, pick 3, pick 4, pick 6, and pick 9.

But no matter what sport you favor, or which bets you prefer, **Money Secrets at the Racetrack** will point you towards profitable plays. Whether you bet $2 a race or $2000, this book will show you exactly how to earn the most profit with the least risk. You'll learn how to uncover winning wagers—and (depending on the size of your bankroll) exactly how much to bet when you find them.

The material in **Money Secrets at the Racetrack** is not just theory. It works. Learn it, use it—and win with it.

PARI-MUTUEL BETTING

Odds are the crowd's opinion, reflected in dollars. To win, you must beat the crowd. Before explaining how to do this, let's take a brief look at the pari-mutuel betting system.

The track, as the money-holder, keeps a commission or takeout. This amount varies from 14% to 26% depending on state or province law, sport, and type of wager. Due to the takeout, the track has little financial interest in which horse wins.

#1	$200	(3-1)
#2	100	(7-1)
#3	60	(12-1)
#4	300	(8-5)
#5	150	(4-1)
#6	25	(31-1)
#7	125	(5-1)
#8	40	(19-1)
Total Pool	$1000	

Let's assume a 20% takeout. No matter who wins, the track will give back about $800, less a few dollars for breakage.

If #4 wins, the payoff will be $5.20:
1. $1000 pool – $200 takeout = $800 payout
2. $ 800 payout – $300 bet on #4 = $500 dividend
3. $ 500 dividend ÷ $300 bet on #4 = $1.666 to 1
4. $1.666 reduced to lower 10 cents for breakage = $1.60

5. $1.60 × $2 + $2 = $5.20 return for $2 bet
6. 150 winning tickets at $5.20 = $780

If #6 wins, the payoff will be $64.00:

1. $1000 pool − $200 takeout = $800 payout
2. $ 800 payout − $25 bet on #6 = $775 dividend
3. $ 775 dividend ÷ $25 bet on #4 = $31.00 to 1
4. no breakage reduction
5. $31.00 × $2 + $2 = $64.00 return for $2 bet
6. 12 1/2 winning tickets at $64.00 = $800

Without the takeout and breakage, the payoffs would have been $6.66 for #4 and $80 for #6. Breakage is computed to the next lower dime in the United States and nickel in Canada; #4 would pay $5.20 in the U.S. and $5.30 in Canada.

Usually, breakage has little effect on high payoffs but a major impact on low ones. For example, let's say a trifecta returns $591.60 for $2; without breakage, the number would have returned, at most, $591.79. However, a $2.20 show payoff might have been slashed from $2.39—reducing the profit by nearly 50%.

Quinella, exacta, trifecta, daily double, pick 3, and pick 4 payoffs are computed in the same way as win bets, although the state/track takeout is frequently higher:

1. Mutuel pool is reduced by the takeout
2. Money bet on winning combination is subtracted
3. Money remaining is divided by amount bet on winning combination
4. This amount, the odds to $1, is reduced by breakage
5. Odds to $1 are multiplied by appropriate minimum, which is then added to calculate final payoff

Take a $100,000 pick 3 pool in which $142 has been bet on the winning combination. This may consist of some $2 tickets, an $11 bet, another for $5, etc. Assuming a 25% takeout, here is the computation:

1. $100,000 − $25,000 = $75,000
2. $ 75,000 − $142 = $74,858
3. $ 74,858 ÷ 142 = $527.16 to 1
4. Breakage reduces odds to $527.10 to 1
5. $527.10 × 2 + 2 = $1056.20

The picture changes with bets that involve a carryover, or consolation payoffs. These plays include the go-for-the-moon bets such as the twin trifecta, pick 6, and pick 9.

Let's take a pick 6 with a 24% takeout, and assume the $100,000 pool is augmented by a $60,000 carryover from the previous day when no one hit all six winners. Furthermore, let's figure that 75% of today's pool and 100% of the carryover pool will be shared by those picking all six, and 25% of today's pool and none of the carryover will go to those picking five winners. If 4 tickets have all six winners today, and 110 tickets have five, here are the payoffs:

For 6 winners

$100,000 (today's pool)
$\underline{-24,000}$ (24% takeout)

$ 76,000 (today's pool after takeout)
$\underline{-19,000}$ (the 25% of today's pool that goes for consolations)

$ 57,000 (for 6 winners from today's pool)
$\underline{+60,000}$ (the carryover from yesterday's pool)

$117,000 (to be awarded for 6 winners including carryover)
$\underline{-\qquad 8}$ (amount bet on the winning combination)

$116,992 \div 8 = $14,624 (the odds to $1)

$ 14,624 \times 2 + $2 = $29,250 (today's payoff for all 6 winners)

For 5 winners

$ 19,000 (the 25% of today's pool that goes for consolations)
$\underline{-\qquad 220}$ (the amount bet on the consolation combinations)

$ 18,780 (to be divided among the consolation winners)

$ 172.60 (today's consolation payoff after breakage)

Note that in this example, more than half the payoff for six winners came solely from the carryover. The track gave out more than $135,000 on a day it took in only $100,000. This is a gambling rarity—a positive-expectation play—and has proven a boon to groups that can afford to lay out large tickets. See the chapter on multiple win exotics for how best to exploit this opportunity.

A multiple win exotic with a 24% takeout is often a much better bet than a win bet with only a 16% takeout. Take a daily double. Assume $50,000 is bet to win in the first race and all the money given back to winning bettors after its completion is plowed back into the second race:

Win Betting = (1st race) $50,000 \times .84 = $42,000
(2nd race) $42,000 \times .84 = $35,280

Daily Double = (2 wins) $50,000 \times .76 = $38,000

Players who bet the daily double with a 24% takeout would receive $38,000 back. Since win bettors are cuffed with the takeout on two races, they would get back only $35,280—even though the bite is just 16%.

The pick 3 is even better:

Win Betting = (1st race) $50,000 × .84 = $42,000
(2nd race) $42,000 × .84 = $35,280
(3rd race) $35,280 × .84 = $29,635
Pick 3 = (3 wins) $50,000 × .76 = $38,000

Despite the larger takeout, pick 3 winners get back 28% more money than they would have had they bet the same horses in the straight pool (assuming the horses have been bet to win and in the pick 3 in the same proportion). Pick 4 winners get back better than 52% more. It's no wonder that sharpies with fat bankrolls prefer to put their money into multiple win exotics.

The two questions you must consider before attacking any pool are:

1. *What are the true odds for this proposition compared with the odds offered?* If the true odds on a horse should be 4-1 (he'll win in this situation one time in five), you'll be a winner if you bet him at 6-1 but a loser if you insist on playing him if he's only 3-1. Bet only when you have an edge.

2. *How likely is this bet to win?* An edge is good, but if you rarely cash, it's not so good:

A $1 slot-machine contains 90 symbols on each column of a three-columned carousel. One symbol on each column is marked "$1 million," which is the amount you collect if all three line up. This will happen once in 729,000 pulls of the machine. Since you will, on average, be betting only $729,000 to win $1 million, this is a positive-expectation play. However, it's a bad one because of the high capital necessary to try. Put $300,000 through the machine and you will typically collect zero. Conceivably, you could have an unlucky run and blow $1.5 million before hitting.

Every bet offered at a racetrack contains a tradeoff between risk vs. reward, and advantages vs. disadvantages. If you bet to show, for example, you rarely suffer a losing streak. If you play the pick 4, breakage is no factor. The pari-mutuel facts are summarized in the chart, which features the most popular bets at North American racetracks.

The charts make certain assumptions, which may not be true in particular cases:

1. True...True odds may be calculated for most bets based on your own odds line. For example, if you bet a $2 pick 3 using your top choices

Comparative Bet Chart

Bet	True	Tote	Win%	Take	20 L	10%S
Win	Yes	Yes	25%	17.0%	0.3%	9
Place	Yes	Est	50%	18.0%	0.0%	4
Show	Yes	Est	70%	18.5%	0.0%	2
Quinella	Yes	Yes	24%	20.3%	0.4%	9
Exacta	Yes	Yes	12%	20.2%	7.8%	19
Trifecta	?	No	8%	25.0%	18.9%	28
Double	Yes	Yes	25%	20.2%	0.3%	9
Pick 3	Yes	No	12%	25.1%	7.8%	19
Pick 4	Yes	No	6%	25.0%	29.0%	38
Pick 6	Yes	No	3%	25.0%	54.4%	76
Pick 9	Yes	No	.2%	25.0%	96.1%	1151
Twin Tri	?	No	.6%	25.0%	88.7%	383

True = Can the true odds be determined?
Tote = Are the crowd's odds posted?
Win% = How often will you collect this bet?
Take = What's the takeout, including estimated breakage?
20L = How often will you lose 20 straight bets?
10%S = 10% of the time, how long will a losing streak last?

only and your odds estimations for them are .50, .40, and .30, the chance of that pick 3's hitting is 6%. True odds are difficult to compute for trifectas and twin trifectas, however, because of the large number of calculations necessary.

2. Tote..."Yes" appears only if odds are posted on a monitor. For place and show, odds depend on which other horses come in, but may be estimated long-term by figuring the horses' percentages of the pools.

3. Win%...A low figure of 25% is listed under win since we assume that you'll often play horses that are not your top choice...Place and show figures are high because nearly all place and show bets should be on low-priced horses...Exacta and trifecta percentages assume you bet several combinations...The daily double, pick 3, pick 4, and pick 9 percentages assume that the player uses 2 horses in each race with their win chances totalling 50%...The pick 6 percentage is a bit higher than these other calculations, since it's assumed people will play larger tickets and hope to hit consolations...The twin trifecta percentage was determined by squar-

ing the trifecta percentage.

4. Take...This column adds estimated breakage to basic takeouts of 16% for win, place, show; 20% for daily double, quinella, exacta; and 25% for pick 3, pick 4, pick 6, pick 9, twin trifecta.

Note the rapid escalation of losing streaks as the percentage of bets collected decreases. If you play the wilder exotic bets, you'd better have a wad of cash under the mattress:

Hitting 8% of your trifectas, 10% of the time you will lose 28 consecutive bets. And because the odds are not posted, it's possible that the one time you hit, the number won't even cover your play in that race.

Cashing 3% of your pick 6's, you will lose 20 in a row more than half the time.

With a typical pick 4 investment of $32 (two horses in each race, and a 50% chance to hit each race), 29% of the time you will lose 20 straight plays, and 10% of the time you will lose 38 in a row. Hitting 6%, your payoffs must average $534 to show a profit.

Assuming you hit a twin trifecta 3 times in every 1000 bets, 10% of the time you will lose 383 plays in a row.

Playing two horses per race with a 50% chance of hitting every race, you'd invest $1024 in a $2 pick 9 with only a 0.2% chance of hitting. And 10% of the time you'd lose 1151 consecutive times, which would wipe out even a $1 million bankroll.

The chart shows that the various types of bets share almost no common characteristics, which is why the strategy for each is different. All, however, can be exploited—and this book will show you how.

DECISIONS VS. SELECTIONS

To make money betting at the track, you must learn about horses, races, and money.

Learn about horses and races to become proficient enough to make a price line, which is your assessment of the relative chances of each horse in a race. Learn about money to best exploit flaws in the public line.

Picking winners is overrated. You can make money at the races even if you pick very few winners. You can lose money even if you pick plenty.

Shopping for bargains, not just picking winners, is the key to making money at racetrack betting. Seek overlays—those animals being sent away at more than their true odds.

How to find the true odds is the greatest challenge of handicapping. But whether you use a computer program, a system, or your own analysis of the past performances, this skill will determine whether you will be able to earn long-term profits at the track. Here is the one rule you must understand:

Analyze chances, rather than attempt to pick winners.

Every race may have a hundred different scripts. In one scenario, a horse who usually breaks slowly suddenly jets from the gate; in another, a speed duel fails to materialize; in a third, the favorite is pinched at the start. Though you get only one chance to play a race, think long term—*if this race were run 100 times, how many times would each horse win?*

Actual odds are set by crowds. And the public is not only often wrong, but its line may career wildly depending on a thousand different factors. For proof, look at the 1986 Kentucky Derby, which was simulcast into more than 40 North American tracks. At each, the local crowd set the odds. Note the variations in the win prices for Ferdinand, who paid $37.40 at Churchill Downs:

Fairplex Park $13.20
Hollywood Park $16.80
Aqueduct.. $37.40
Hialeah.. $63.20

At the southern California tracks, where Ferdinand had raced and where trainer Charles Whittingham and jockey Willie Shoemaker were magic names, the horse paid 5-1 and 7-1. Yet at Hialeah, the same horse paid more than 30-1. (Not that the southern California players are sharper than anyone else. When Washington shipper Saratoga Passage took the Norfolk Stake at Santa Anita in 1987, he paid $27 to win at the track but only $12.60 at little Yakima Meadows in Washington.)

Conclusion? Every crowd is different. Every day is different. Every race is different. And *you never know when the public is going to hand you a bargain.*

Let's take a typical race in which you like Speedy Sam best but figure that Wily Willie is the one to beat. Assume further that you are an expert handicapper and that your line accurately reflects the chances of every horse. You estimate that Speedy Sam has a 50% chance to win and Wily Willie a 20% chance.

Stated another way, if this race were run 100 times, you think that Speedy Sam would win 50 and Wily Willie 20. Break-even payoffs, therefore, would be even-money or $4 for Speedy Sam and 4-1 or $10 for Wily Willie. Over the 100-race series, look at the differing returns you'd get, depending on the tote odds:

A.	Speedy Sam	4-5	−$20.00	
	Wily Willie	7-2	−$20.00	No play.
B.	Speedy Sam	9-5	+$80.00	
	Wily Willie	3-1	−$40.00	Bet Speedy Sam.

| C. Speedy Sam | 3-5 | −$40.00 | |
| Wily Willie | 8-1 | +$160.00 | Bet Wily Willie. |

| D. Speedy Sam | 7-2 | +$250.00 | |
| Wily Willie | 9-1 | +$200.00 | Bet both. |

Even though Speedy Sam has a far greater chance than Wily Willie to win the race—and hence, the individual bet—at times he is a much worse investment. This indicates that sometimes, you will not play your top choice in a race. Or your second choice. Or your third.

You will play only when there is value.

Some players want to bet their pick, no matter what. Instead, think value—which means that your decisions may not be the same as your selections.

At times, your top choice will win without you. But if he does not offer value, don't play him. And it doesn't matter how much you like him.

Don't look for winners. Instead, *seek the best bet for the odds*. Sometimes it's a win bet on one horse. Other times it's a place or show bet. Or seven exacta combinations.

Value in racetrack betting is similar to value in any other endeavor involving pricing. Some examples:

a. A new car costs $21,000 at Dealer A. Another make, with some of the same features, sells for $18,500 at Dealer B.
b. Two houses appear equal in size and general appearance. One costs $100,000 but is in a less desirable neighborhood than the other, which is listed at $160,000.
c. A stereo system is priced at $4,000. Another costs only $1,200 but the quality is not as good.

Price is never the only consideration. The question in each of these examples is how does the price of one item compare with the price of another *for the value offered*? Maybe the resale worth is much higher on the $21,000 car, or the company has a better warranty; then again, maybe the $18,500 car is a far superior value. Perhaps the two houses appear similar, but the $160,000 home is the cheapest house in a terrific area where values are skyrocketing, and the $100,000 home is in a deteriorating neighborhood where values are sinking. Or the $1,200 stereo, though its quality is inferior to the $4,000 system, may still deliver adequate fidelity at a bargain price.

Value is price vs. worth. Every price must be compared with every worth—and vice versa.

Demand that the crowd offer you a price at least 50% above what you consider a fair price for a horse or combination. If you do not receive at least a 50% bonus, do not play.

Why 50%? Why not 10% or 100%? From thousands of bets over many years, I've found that a 50% bonus on every bet will yield somewhere between 8% and 10% profit on total money invested. Any bonus lower than 50% will result in a loss. A higher bonus requirement won't yield enough plays.

Why doesn't a 50% bonus yield a 50% edge? Several factors combine to reduce profit.

First, *a 50% bonus is not the same as a 50% edge.* Your edge is:

Probability of win × odds − probability of loss

A 3-1 shot that goes off at 9-2 offers an edge of 37.5%:
$$(.25) \ (4.5) - .75 \ = \ .375$$
A 1-1 shot that goes off at 3-2 offers an edge of just 25%:
$$(.50) \ (1.5) - .50 \ = \ .250$$
A 50% bonus always offers an edge of at least 22%, though the edge never reaches 50% unless the horse goes off at far above a 50% bonus.

Second, *the odds will often drop after we bet,* even if we play close to post time. Let's say we make a certain horse 2-1. For a 50% bonus, he'd have to go off at least 3-1. With one minute to post, he's 3-1. We bet. But just as the race goes off, he drops to 5-2, only a slight edge. By demanding at least 50%, we insure that the vast majority of our bets will still be overlays of at least some amount at post time.

Third, *every bet we make has a certain impact on the odds.* The smaller the handle and the larger our bet, the greater the influence. At a small track during the middle of the week, for example, a $10 exacta bet on a long-priced combination may cut the price by 20%.

Fourth, *our own line—no matter how good we get—will never be quite as accurate as the public's.* Underlays, unfortunately, always do better than overlays. For example, horses we make even money may well win 50% of the time—but those that wind up going off at 3-5 might win 56%

while those who wind up at 3-2 might win only 42%. By allowing for errors, we give ourselves a safety margin.

Our procedure, then, is this:

1. *Analyze the chances* of every horse in the race (e.g., Fleet Guy has a 25% chance to win, Quick Gal a 20% chance, etc.).

2. *Determine fair odds* using the table in the chapter, "Making The Line" (e.g., Fleet Guy would be 3-1, Quick Gal 4-1, etc.).

3. Bet to win any horse that is at least *50% above the line.* For place, show, quinellas, exactas, and daily doubles, use your line with our charts in those sections of the book to decide whether to play. For multiple win exotics such as pick 3's and pick 6's, use your line to help construct your tickets.

BEATING THE PUBLIC

Picking winners at the races is no big deal. Just bet all the public favorites and you'll cash one-third of your bets. You'll also lose your money. To win, you must find overlays.

Our opposition is the public. Every bet we make is a contest between our perception and theirs. If we can find enough discrepancies between our opinion and the crowd's—and if we're right often enough—we'll win.

How much better must we be than the crowd to succeed? Battling a 20% grab for takeout and breakage, we must be 25% better than the crowd to break even $(1.00 \div .80 - 1.00 = .250)$. With a 23% takeout, we must be nearly 30% better $(1.00 \div .77 - 1.00 = .298)$.

The crowd consists of many elements. The vast majority are casual fans, many of whom can barely read a *Daily Racing Form* (if they buy one at all). They bet on hunches and numbers, or follow crude, ill-informed handicapping theories.

Though this group is large in number, it is only a partial influence. A small circle of big-money regulars heavily affects the pools. A survey at Aqueduct Racetrack not long ago, for example, showed that 42% of the money is bet by only 1.5% of the players. And it's this clique—which includes some high-rolling casual fans but is also made up of professional gamblers, expert handicappers and racing insiders—that is tougher to beat.

Before the advent of cash-sell machines, you had to bet at windows of particular denominations; e.g., $10 win, $2 show, etc. Surveys at the time showed that players at the big-money windows far outperformed those at the $2 windows. Recent surveys have shown that late money outdoes early money—and most big bets go in close to post time.

Much of this sharp late flow is adjustment money, correcting for the casual fans' early play. It figures that if experts feel that Zippy Zipster should be 6-5 and with three minutes to post he's 5-2, the boys will pound. Conversely, if he's overplayed at 3-5, the smart money will lay off him and go to someone who offers better value.

At some small tracks, this "smart money" might come from only a single bettor. And mob psychology sometimes takes over after a big punch on a horse. If an animal hovers around 3-1 and then, with a minute till post, skips the 5-2 mark to drop directly to 2-1, many bettors consider this a providential sign and then follow the hot money, driving the horse's price down even further.

How big a bet does it take to move a number? Far less than you might think. Let's say a track handles $500,000 a day, or about $50,000 a race. Of this amount, 50% might be bet in the exotic pool, 35% to win, 10% to place, and 5% to show. Since most money is bet relatively late, with five minutes to post there may be only $7,000 in the win pool. A horse listed at 20-1 on the board has less than $300 bet on him. A single $200 bet may knock the odds down to 12-1. In the exacta pool, if a number is returning $400 for $2 with five minutes to go, a mere $25 exacta play will slice the payoff to perhaps $320; if three guys independently decide to play $20 each on the number, adios overlay.

It's much worse at a minor track. Let's say Obscure Downs handles only $125,000 on a winter Tuesday. There is so little in these pools that a single $250 win bet or $50 exacta play will move virtually any number —even an 8-5 shot.

While there may be "inside" money on a race—cash bet by knowledgeable horsemen who know of a secret workout three days before the race, or are aware that a certain favorite is lame, or that tonight is a go after an easy debut race—there is no simple way to detect its presence. You cannot tell who is responsible for an odds drop on a horse, no matter what a book or system may claim.

Some insiders, if their horse is expected to be a favorite, chunk it in at the beginning of the betting period, figuring that the ridiculously low posted odds (say, 2-5 on a horse who figures to be 8-5) will discourage bettors. Others send in the money slowly throughout so as not to attract attention. Others wait until the last moment, hoping to crush the price just seconds before post time so that other players may not react. At tracks that permit bet cancellations, some tricksters make a big bet early on another horse to fool the public, then cancel it and send in the money on their original pick. Some insiders bet with bookmakers, or have beards wager for them.

Many horsemen bet rarely or never. Others tell everybody in the county that their horse looks good tonight. But it really doesn't matter most of the time—an inordinate number of hotties manage to lose, further clouding the picture.

My most fervent hope at the track is that the horses I like will get absolutely no tote action whatsoever. It's no thrill to spend an hour finding an apparent longshot who, at trackside, is banged down to 7-5. Who needs him? I'd rather play someone who is getting less action than I think he deserves—not more.

There's always the temptation to follow the hot money, particularly on a horse with no form, on the theory that somebody knows something. And, at times, somebody does. In the long run, though, following your own opinion is the way to make money at the track—if your opinion is good enough.

We compete against a crowd that is constantly adjusting and correcting its earlier odds. And it's a tough opponent. As a whole, the public is a good predictor of race results. More than half a dozen studies, involving tens of thousands of races, have found these conclusions:

1. *The lower the odds, the more likely a horse is to win.* The surveys show that 3-5 shots win more than 4-5 shots, 9-2 shots do better than 5-1 shots, etc. The likeliest method of picking the winner is simply to play the public favorite in every race.

2. *The public overbets longshots and underbets favorites.* Betting every public favorite, you'd lose half the takeout; betting every 50-1 shot, you'd lose far more than the takeout. When you play longshots, you're getting the worst of both worlds—higher risk and lesser return.

Though the crowd does pick plenty of winners, the fans also make plenty of mistakes. It's not necessary to win every race, or even a majority. Since we demand a 50% bonus for our plays, all we need to make money betting races is to find small errors. We probe the crowd's line for vulnerable spots to attack.

For example, we make a horse 4-1, meaning we think it will win this race 20% of the time. The crowd dismisses him at 9-1. Even if he wins only 14% of the time—meaning we were overly optimistic in our assessment—we will still show a profit.

Though the public is not a bad handicapper, most of their top choices lose. And being able to bet against a false favorite is one of your biggest edges. While there are dozens of reasons why a favorite might lose, five are among the most common predictors of a poor performance. Recognize these deficiences and you're well on your way to throwing out overbet favorites:

1. *Misleading lines.* The horse has gotten lucky trips or been sucked along to fast times. Unsophisticated players think this horse is better than he actually is.

2. *Tough spot.* He's a dog who does best from middle posts and today he's drawn the rail. Or he's a non-leaving pacer from the outside. Though he may be best on class, the race doesn't set up for him.

3. *Poor form.* The horse has been idle awhile and shows no strong workout pattern. Or he's a trotter who, after four straight wins, threw in a horrible, no-excuse loss last week.

4. *Quitter or rat.* A quitter often stops despite favorable fractions, and a rat refuses to pass his opponents except by accident. Even if he raced well last week, it's likely he'll revert to his basic nature today.

5. *Weak jockey/driver.* The horse appears best but is being handled by someone who doesn't win many races.

But it's not just bad favorites we look for. Our goal is to ferret out value wherever it lies. Sometimes there's value because the fans overplay the favorite, or another horse you're not fond of. Other times the fans will underplay someone for other reasons.

How can you tell if a horse is an overlay (playable) or an underlay (not playable)? Simply *make a line for every race that interests you.*

Not every race will. Some may feature eight dogs whose last race was a schooling race. A thoroughbred allowance might offer two first-timers from France, a class horse that hasn't raced in six months, and a sharp shipper—too many questions. Another could be a $3000 claimer in which no one in the field has ever gone forward—too boring. Or a race might be so contentious and confusing that any line would be mere guesswork. You'll also skip some races because of doubts about intentions (such as a maiden pace in which half the field may merely be trying to stay classified).

But for every other race—and that will normally mean 80% of the races on a typical card—make a line. This numerical expression of your opinion will show you exactly which horse, or horses, are playable.

You may not want to make a line. Math bores you. Line-making bores you. But be aware of this: If you make lines religiously, you will not only improve your handicapping, but you will learn exactly how good a handicapper you are. The reason for this is that the two most common methods players use to assess their own ability—win percentage and profits/losses—are completely misleading.

Win percentage means nothing unless it's mated with prices. If you hit 50% of your bets but your payoffs average only $3.20, you're a loser; if your top choices win only 20% but average $13.00, you're a winner.

Strangely enough, profit or loss means very little also, particularly when a high percentage of your dollars are invested in longshot plays such as trifectas or double quinellas. Take two handicappers, Huey and Louie, each of whom bets $10,000 a year. Last year Huey collected $11,000 for a 10% profit, while Louie collected only $8,500 for a 15% loss. Is Huey a superior handicapper while Louie is a loser? I don't know, because there was a $2,500 trifecta in which Huey's third horse beat Louie's third horse by an inch. One inch the other way and Huey's results would have been switched with Louie's.

So let's get back to the one method which will determine—for sure—how well you handicap the races. It's simply this:

Make your own odds line for every race that interests you, then check the results at the end of 200 races. Record not only the odds you assigned each horse, but also whether the horse was overlaid or underlaid.

Did the horses you made 1-1 actually win 50% of their starts? That's a good start—but if your 1-1 shots who went off at 3-5 won 60% and those who went off at 2-1 won only 25%, you'll have to keep practicing your oddsmaking. And that's the whole idea—to learn how well you handicap, and to improve your skills to determine true values.

MAKING THE LINE

The odds we assign are based on one premise: *If this race were run 100 times, how many would each horse win?*

In reality, this race is going to be run only once and there is going to be only one winner. But by assigning chances, we force ourselves to reflect on every possible factor and come to conclusions.

At the track, few players make up an odds line. Most express their opinions vaguely:
"I like the 4 a little bit."
"It looks close between the 3, 6, and 8."
"The 5 looks good, but the price is a little short."

We don't want vagueness. If you like the 4 "a little bit," what exactly does that mean? At 6-1? As the probable winner and playable at 6-5? Enough to make a large bet on him?

If you don't make a line, you won't be able to quickly determine whether a bet offers value. And it puts you in league with the pathetic souls who narrow the race to six contenders, bet one of the losers, and then say "I shudda had him" when one of the others wins.

Making an odds line does several things for you:
• It requires you to quantify your opinion, so that you're considering not just one horse, but how that horse relates to everyone else.
• It is a test of handicapping ability which can be measured over

years, in that you can survey the performance of all your 2-1 shots, all your 6-1 shots, etc.

• It enables you to find overlays in win, place, show, quinella, exacta, and daily double pools, and to calculate exactly what your chances are of winning a particular pick 3, pick 4, or pick 6.

If you've never made an odds line before, it will take you some time initially. As with any skill, the more you practice, the swifter you'll get. In the middle of a season, it normally takes me no more than five minutes to not only mark the *Form* but to compute my odds line for that race. The entire card rarely takes more than an hour.

As the total chances of all contestants equal 100%, so must our odds line. (The track's line, which allows for takeout, may equal 125% or more —ours must always equal 100%, never higher.) Here is the odds-percentage table to use:

Odds Percentage Table

1-10	90.91	4-1	20.00
1-5	83.33	9-2	18.19
2-5	71.42	5-1	16.67
1-2	66.67	6-1	14.29
3-5	62.50	7-1	12.50
4-5	55.56	8-1	11.11
1-1	50.00	9-1	10.00
6-5	45.45	10-1	9.09
7-5	41.67	11-1	8.33
3-2	40.00	12-1	7.69
8-5	38.46	15-1	6.25
9-5	35.71	20-1	4.76
2-1	33.33	25-1	3.85
5-2	28.57	30-1	3.23
3-1	25.00	50-1	1.96
7-2	22.22	99-1	1.00

If we think that Horse A would win this race half the time, we look under 50% in the table and mark Horse A at even money. If we think his main rival, B, would win 25% of the time, we make him 3-1. We continue this process all the way through the field.

Odds are merely a numerical way to express chances. Odds of 4-1, for example, mean the horse has one chance in five—20%—of winning. You won't need to do so, because the table lists the percentages, but here is how to calculate them using a 7-2 shot as an example:
1. Add both numbers (7 + 2 = 9)
2. Divide second number in odds by total (2 ÷ 9 = .222)
3. Convert result to whole number per cents (22.2%)

Working the other way, let's say you use a mathematical system that gives a certain horse 23.7% of the points:
1. Divide 100 by appropriate percentage (100 ÷ 23.7 = 4.219)
2. To get odds to $1, subtract 1 (4.219 − 1 = 3.219)
3. Use closest higher odds (closest to 3.219 is 7-2)

Every handicapping factor gets its due in your line. Everything positive makes a horse more likely to win, and thus lowers his odds. Everything negative makes him more likely to lose, and thus raises his odds.

Your numbers will reflect only what you think the chances are of each horse's winning the race. Unlike the morning linemaker, you have no interest in predicting what the public will do. Unlike a Nevada sports-betting linemaker, you're not trying to come up with a number that will attract equal action on both sides.

The only thing you are concerned about is expressing your opinion about a race numerically. Like a horse, give him low odds. Hate him, give him high odds.

When compiling the line, start with the most likely winner, proceed to the second choice, drop to the third choice, etc., in order. You can work in one of two ways:
1. *Assign chances and then convert them to odds.* For example, you give A a 50% chance to win, B 20%, etc. To convert these numbers to odds, use the table. Or, if you prefer, use this formula: Odds = 1 ÷ Probability − 1. If you give a horse a 30% chance to win, for instance, the math would be 1 ÷ .30 − 1 or $2.33 to 1. The table is quicker and should cover most possibilities.
2. *Use the odds directly from the table*: A 1-1, B 4-1, etc. Use whole numbers rather than decimals for your first, tentative total (e.g., if you make a horse 6-1, use 14 rather than 14.29). When you get close to 100, then include the decimals to be certain that your total doesn't exceed 100. I stop when my number reaches 99 and a fraction.

I use the second method, since I carry the conversion numbers in my head. But whichever method you use, the procedure is the same: Give everyone odds, add the totals, then adjust your numbers. If your total exceeds 100%, increase the odds of some horses (e.g., raise one horse from 5-2 to 3-1 and another from 6-1 to 7-1). If it's too low, cut the odds of some horses (e.g., drop one from 8-5 to 3-2, another from 9-2 to 4-1, etc.). Keep the odds-percentage table by your side as you work.

Here would be a typical first-draft line on a race:

#1................8-5
#2...............10-1
#3................6-1
#4..............50-1
#5................7-2
#6...............12-1
#7...............15-1
#8................8-1

Our total comes to 111%—too high. So we fiddle, reviewing the race to increase the odds on some horses while pondering our rank order. At times we'll raise the favorite, other times the least likely winners, often a combination—there's no set pattern. Does #1 have some negatives which would cause us to raise his odds? Are #6 and #7 really that close? Should #3 be longer than 6-1? After adjustment, our new line may be:

#1   9-5 (formerly 8-5)
#2   11-1 (formerly 10-1)
#3   7-1 (formerly 6-1)
#4   100-1 (formerly 50-1)
#5   7-2 (same)
#6   15-1 (formerly 12-1)
#7   20-1 (formerly 15-1)
#8   10-1 (formerly 8-1)

Note that we kept one horse (#5) the same and moved another (#8) two points on the line. In some races, we need adjust only one horse; occasionally our preliminary line will add up to 99% and we won't need to make any changes.

These three sample races, entirely different in their makeup, show some of the possibilities in line-making.

In I, we have a lukewarm favorite, two solid second choices, and a few outside possibilities. In II, we have one powerful favorite and a fairly open battle for second. In III, we can't pick a favorite (#1 and #3 wind

I	II	III
#1 8-1	#1 1-2	#1 4-1
#2 30-1	#2 25-1	#2 7-1
#3 5-1	#3 100-1	#3 4-1
#4 100-1	#4 12-1	#4 6-1
#5 9-2	#5 25-1	#5 9-1
#6 10-1	#6 200-1	#6 30-1
#7 15-1	#7 9-1	#7 200-1
#8 100-1	#8 20-1	#8 11-1
#9 2-1	#9 100-1	#9 8-1

up co-favored on our line) and we give seven horses a decent chance.

Because every race is different, no single model is applicable to all of them. Remain flexible.

When you have stable entries, give each horse points on your line, then add them to get the entry's total and assign odds based on that total. For example, if in a three-horse entry you make one 3-1, a second 5-1, and a third 15-1, the entry would receive 25.00 + 16.67 + 6.25, for a total of 47.92 points out of your 100-point pie. The closest lower total on the chart would make the entry 6-5, even though you don't like any individual member better than 3-1.

At the harness races, a difficult horse to make a line on is the breaker, especially the good trotter who figures to either win or gallop. When making a line for a trot race, assume everyone will stay flat. Then adjust for the likelihood of each horse's going off-stride. For instance, you figure that Somolli Swifty has a 50% chance to win if he stays flat but he breaks one-fourth of the time. That would give him a $.50 \times .75$ or 37.5% chance of winning. His odds on your line should be 9-5, not 1-1.

In a race where tote action will be the key to a horse's chances (e.g., a gambling stable has a well-bred 2-year-old who was a nowhere 40-1 in its debut), make your line as if the mystery horse is a throwout but put the word "board" next to its odds. This will alert you that any heavy tote action on the animal means you should re-evaluate the race—and possibly not play it at all. It costs nothing to pass a questionable race.

Make your lines long before the first race. Otherwise, an early score (or setback) may mess up your thinking. The calm before your opening bet is the best time to make your lines. If post time is 1 p.m., either work on your line in the morning (after calling to get the late scratches), or arrive at the track by 11:30 a.m. to allow time to finish your work.

After you've finished your preliminary line, make late changes based on scratches, jockey switches, especially sharp (or dull) paddock appearances, or (for later races) a possible track bias. That gives you the final line—the numbers that will tell you if the crowd offers value in that race.

Use your numbers to find overlays in various pools where TV monitors or the toteboard display possible payoffs, including win, place, show, quinella, exacta, and daily double. For bets that require a sequence of winners (e.g., pick 3's or pick 6's), use the numbers to evaluate whether to play based on pool size vs. likely amount of return.

Let's look at a typical odds line, checking only whether anyone should be bet to win:

Horse	Chances	My Odds	Tote Odds	Overlay?
A	33	2-1	6-5	No
B	25	3-1	3-1	No
C	20	4-1	8-1	Yes
D	10	9-1	9-2	No
E	5	19-1	7-1	No
F	4	24-1	22-1	No
G	2	49-1	18-1	No
H	1	99-1	30-1	No

My bet is C, even though he's only my third choice and I expect to lose this bet 80% of the time. If this race were run 100 times, I believe that A would win 33 and C only 20. On one hundred $2 bets, A at 6-5 would return only $145.20 (33 × $4.40) for a loss of $54.80 while C at 8-1 would return $360 (20 × $18) for a profit of $160.

And it's profit we're after. *Our goal at the track is to make money*, not just brag that we picked the winner. Here are two more races, with the recommended win bets:

Horse	Chances	My Odds	Tote Odds	Overlay?
I	12	7-1	4-1	No
J	35	9-5	3-1	Yes
K	10	9-1	5-1	No
L	3	30-1	20-1	No
M	7	12-1	7-1	No
N	15	6-1	5-1	No
O	10	9-1	9-2	No
P	8	11-1	7-1	No

My play here is J, my first choice, even though he has the lowest odds in the field. I think he should be a stronger favorite. No one else is overlaid.

Horse	Chances	My Odds	Tote Odds	Overlay?
Q	4	25-1	15-1	No
R	15	6-1	11-1	Yes
S	3	30-1	12-1	No
T	40	3-2	4-5	No
U	22	7-2	6-1	Yes
V	2	50-1	13-1	No
W	1	99-1	25-1	No
X	9	10-1	5-1	No
Y	3	30-1	35-1	No
Z	1	99-1	70-1	No

In this race, two horses (R and U) are bettable. Y isn't 50% over the line (and has probably been lined out anyway). My top choice, T, is way overbet to win.

Later chapters show how to use your lines at the track for bets in all pools. For further study, Mark Cramer's book, *The Odds On Your Side,* is devoted strictly to line-making at the thoroughbreds and includes many more examples.

Overlays are not necessarily longshots. Although I rarely bet horses below even money, I might play a 1-1 shot if I make him 3-5 on my line. And a 70-1 shot could well be an underlay if I make him 200-1.

On a typical day, about four or five races offer a playable win overlay, usually not more than one per race. That means that more than 90% of all starters will offer no betting value whatsoever. No wonder almost everybody loses.

The key, of course, is figuring out which horses are the true overlays. I say Champ Hanover should be 4-1 but my neighbor thinks he's no better than 12-1. If Champ goes off at 8-1, I'll bet him and my pal won't. If I am to make money, my opinion must be more accurate than that of the crowd at large.

Odds are made by human beings, and there's no accounting for taste. Don't stand in awe of the crowd—a majority voted for Nixon and Agnew. Do your own handicapping and learn enough to have confidence in your own opinion.

Some players are paralyzed by fear. They see a horse at a big price and think the worst. Something is wrong with the animal. Or the stable isn't trying. Convincing themselves that things are not as they seem, they pass the race—and watch helplessly as the overlay runs off at 8-1.

In racing, things usually are as they seem. Slow horses don't suddenly turn fast, and fast horses don't suddenly turn slow—at least not very often.

You never know when the crowd is going to fall asleep. The public may go eight straight races picking the logical favorite, and then they'll make a glaring error.

When that happens, the typical player thinks his handicapping has gone awry. Perhaps it has. Often, though, the public is simply wrong. But the bettor who believes in the collective wisdom now faces a dilemma. Should he bet the apparent overlay? Should he go to the steam horse? Should he skip the race altogether? Doubt takes over—and doubt is your greatest enemy. You must believe in your own opinion. The player who thinks nothing of betting $200 on a 6-5 shot because the crowd agrees with him but cuts his bet to $10 if his pick is 8-1 because the crowd doesn't share his opinion is a certain loser.

Merely determining that Horse A will usually beat Horse B is not the end-all of handicapping. If A has topped B five out of seven lately but is 3-5 while B is 25-1, the slower horse might well be the better bet. To succeed at racetrack betting, learn the art of comparison—comparing a horse's odds with its true chances.

And *the best way to do that is to make a line.*

Linemaking is tedious, though it gets easier with practice. At the beginning, it may take 15 minutes to make one line come out right. And at times you feel as though your brain will explode if you have to make one more fine distinction, such as whether to make a horse 4-1 or 9-2.

Nonetheless, making an accurate price line will open a new world for you. No longer will you think in terms of picking a winner. Instead, you'll be concentrating on finding the best bet for the odds—and that is the road to long-term profit. Never again will you say, "How could that winner go off at such a big price?"—because you'll have him.

At the very least, *make an odds line for your contenders.* I always start my analysis of a race by crossing off the horses I don't think can win. In a nine-horse race, this number may vary from eight (such as in a stakes race where the favorite looks like a solid 1-5 shot) to only one or two. About 15% of the time, a horse I line out wins—meaning my contenders win 85%.

To stay on the conservative side, give your contenders 80% and assume your lineouts will win 20%. Do not try to separate your lineouts. This will reduce your handicapping time while not appreciably changing your results. Your contenders-only line may look like this:

> A—25% (3-1)
> B—lineout
> C—lineout
> D—18% (9-2)
> E—22% (7-2)
> F—lineout
> G—lineout
> H—14% (6-1)

While you like A best, it's possible you might bet on D, E, or H. Exactas using any combination of these four are possible. By limiting the total points to 80 (rather than 100), you recognize that a certain percentage of races will be won by horses you don't like—and thus you allow for surprises. Here's another contenders-only line:

> I —lineout
> J —7-5
> K—lineout
> L —9-1
> M—lineout
> N—4-1
> O —lineout
> P —lineout
> Q —11-1

The advantage of doing a contenders-only line is that it's both faster and easier. The disadvantages are that it's not as precise as a full line, it's not as accurate (sometimes your contenders deserve 95% of a line, other times only 70%), and by not separating your lineouts you won't be able to use them in the two-hole in exactas. Still, making a contenders-only line is far better than making no line at all.

I cannot emphasize too strongly the importance of making a line. It will force you to think seriously about each race—and all the strategies in this book assume that you will make a line to express your opinion about a race.

THE TRUTH ABOUT MONEY

Proper money management, a wise guy once explained, is betting the maximum on your winners and the minimum on your losers.

It is possible to be the best handicapper in the universe and still lose money if you don't handle your cash correctly. Example: A man hits 99% winners. Unfortunately, he bets 100% of his capital on every play. As soon as he misses, he's broke.

Four items of advice summarize the matter:
1. Keep records of all bets and expenses.
2. Do not overbet in relation to your bankroll.
3. Bet more when the value is greater.
4. Bet within your emotional threshhold.

I have seen countless systems that purport to turn losing series of bets into profits through skillful bet variation. All these methods, however, depend on no extraordinary strings of losers. Unfortunately, a baby may be due and the rent may be due, but a winner is never due.

Even when you play the game with an advantage—and a professional bettor may realistically expect to win 8% to 10% on each invested dollar —your losing streaks will astonish you. Playing five races a day five times a week, it is no big deal to lose for months at a time.

Anyone who tells you different is lying.

A mathematical principle known as *standard deviation* shows the range of possible wins for any betting method. Simplifying things by assuming the payoffs will remain constant, it's calculated by taking the square root of this three-part total: number of races × win probability × loss probability.

Let's say a place betting method hits 49% winners at a $4.20 average mutuel for a 2.9% return on investment. The standard deviation for 100 races is 5 (calculated by taking the square root of $100 \times .49 \times .51$). Your totals will fall within one standard deviation 68% of the time (44-54 wins), within two 95% of the time (39-59 wins), and within three nearly 100% of the time (34-64).

For a 10,000-race series, your expected profit for $2 bets is $580. But your standard deviation is 50 wins. That means that instead of hitting the expected 4900 wins out of 10,000 bets, three standard deviations could place you as low as 4750—which would turn you into a net loser.

Consider this profound, horrifying truth—*you can be a winning player, with an edge on every wager, and bet on 10,000 races only to wind up behind.*

Scary, huh?

This brings up an even worse problem. Suppose you hit 49 of your first 100 races and bet as if you would continue to hit this percentage forever —but on the next 100 you fall to only 42. Or maybe your real percentage is only 38%, and both the first two sequences were above average.

That's why you need long, long, long workouts of betting results before you can develop correct strategies. And the lower your win percentage, the longer workouts you need. Take a trifecta result in which you play one $2 ticket on 120 trifectas and hit six at an average mutuel of $52. With a healthy 30% profit margin, things look promising. Moving along to a 500-race series, the standard deviation is 4.87 (the square root of the total of $500 \times .05 \times .95$). That means while on average you'd hit 25 trifectas, hitting only 10 out of 500 is within the three standard-deviations range—and that would mean a nearly 50% loss.

How many races would you need to realistically check this trifecta method (which, remember, yielded a 30% profit margin after 120 plays)? Dick Mitchell, who's written several excellent books that feature money management, suggests in *Thoroughbred Handicapping as an Invest-*

ment this formula:

$$N = (W) \times (L) \times (Z \div E) \times (Z \div E)$$

Z is defined as a certain constant (1.645 for 90% confidence, 2.575 for 99% confidence), and E is the maximum allowable error in win percentage. In the trifecta example, we have a win percentage of 5% (for a 30% profit margin) and could decrease it to 4% (for a 4% profit margin). Thus to validate our method at the 99% confidence level, we'd have to keep our percentage and average mutuel up for 3149 plays—even with this alleged 30% edge:

$$(.05) \times (.95) \times (2.575 \div .01) \times (2.575 \div .01) = 3149$$

In the short run, of course, almost any result is conceivable. On any particular day or week, a player might do weird things (back-wheeling his fifth choice in the exacta, going 8×8 in a daily double, playing four horses in a race, etc.) and wind up with a net profit. But we're looking for lifetime success—not flukes. And that means we spend our days at the racetrack seeking value.

Before delving into how to find value, let's cast off some of the myths that losing players believe. Take the old chestnut, "You can beat a race but you can't beat the races." This is a rationalization for losers. And to losers, it's true—they can't beat the races.

Actually, the opposite is true. You can't beat a race, but you can beat the races. If you play only overlays—horses going off at more than their "correct" odds—you must beat the races.

Losers think of selecting the winner and beating a race. Professionals think of betting for value and beating the races.

Here's a list of some of the more common betting falsehoods:
- You can beat a race, but you can't beat the races.
- Alter your bet size based on your last result.
- Bet your top pick, but only at 2-1 or higher.
- Don't bet place or show, except savers.
- Don't bet two horses in one race.
- Box or baseball your exactas.
- A real pro bets only one or two races a day.
- Don't mess with trifectas or pick 6's.
- A clever plan turns flat-bet losses into profits.

All these beliefs are wrong. Let's explore why.

"Alter your bet size based on your last result."
This includes any plan to raise or lower your bet after a win, or a loss. Among this group: "Bet more when you're winning because you're playing with the track's money." "Raise your bet after a loss because you're due to win." "Bet a constant percentage of your bankroll." You never know whether your next bet, or series, is going to win or lose. *Bet size depends on your win percentage and advantage*, not on whether you hammered the double.

"Bet your top pick, but only at 2-1 or higher."
This fallacy fails to consider *what chance you give your top pick in a particular race*. All top choices are not equal. Not long ago, I reviewed some statistics for four harness meetings and found my first choice won 38% of the time. But while horses I made 1-1 or below won 53% of their starts, those I made exactly 2-1 won only 28%—and it was from this group that most of the higher-priced horses came.

"Don't bet place or show, except savers."
There is *no such thing as insurance*—every bet either wins or loses on its own merits. If a horse offers value to place or show, then play him, regardless of whether you bet him to win. It's even possible (though rare) to bet one horse to win and another to show. The backup slots are simply two more possible areas of profit.

"Don't bet two horses in one race."
You wouldn't think of betting only one $2 bet in the trifecta or exacta, so why restrict yourself on the win end? You must, however, *deduct the cost of the losing bet* from your determination about whether a race offers value. If you do play two horses in a race, stick with those going off at 3-1 or higher. Otherwise, if you back two horses at 2-1, for example, you stand to collect only $6 for a $4 bet—and if you ordinarily don't take below even money for one horse, then don't for two.

"Box or baseball your exactas."
The only time to do this is when you are getting the same *overlay value on each ticket*, which happens occasionally in boxes (two horses) but rarely in baseballs (three or more horses). Boxing and baseballing come from the same mindset as searching for winners—the myth that collecting on an individual race means much in the long run.

"A real pro bets only one or two races a day."
While I don't know any professional who bets every race, most play

whenever they feel they have an edge—and that may be as often as six or seven times per card. The edge might be a single exacta overlay on their second and third choices, or a show bet, or a daily double with the first-race favorite. But while a pro may make one or two prime plays a day, he rarely sits on his hands the rest of the time.

"Don't mess with trifectas or pick 6's."

On the contrary, *the bets with the biggest payoffs offer your major chance to crush.* While the takeout for these bets sometimes exceeds 25%, so many fans throw away money on hopeless combinations that a good handicapper can do well in these exotic bets. And pick 6's with big carryovers offer the heavily capitalized professional his best edge of all.

"A clever plan turns flat-bet losses into profits."

The sad truth is, *if you can't stay in the black making flat bets, you can't make money in the long run through any other betting plan.* No progression, due-column, cancellation, or any other scheme can perform mathematical alchemy on a losing method. The way to turn flat-bet losses into profits is to improve your handicapping.

So much for what not to do. The rest of this book will dwell on the positives—exactly how to handle every type of bet that's available at the track.

KEEPING RECORDS

There's no point in devising detailed betting strategies unless you're a winning player. And the only way to discover the truth about your play is to keep records.

You can't run a business without a set of books, yet I'm constantly amazed by the number of players who have no real idea of how they do at the track. Perhaps it's that most players lose—and nobody likes to have defeat rubbed in his face. Still, haphazard records lead to haphazard conclusions.

Short samples are useless and misleading. An example: In their book *Racetrack Betting*, authors Peter Asch and Richard E. Quandt examined the performance of a certain computer handicapping program. In 103 plays, the program showed a 41% profit. But the sample included a $134 winner; take that horse away and the program compiled a 25% loss. So what was the truth—was the program a solid winner, a horrible loser that couldn't even match the takeout, or what? Darned if I know—the sample was too tiny.

The greater the variation in payoffs, the larger the sample size you need to draw fair conclusions. If you're checking a show-betting system whose payoffs average $2.40, for instance, a sample of 100 plays would probably be adequate. But if you're studying a trifecta method where the payoffs vary from $16 to $16,000, even a study of 4000 plays may not give you enough information from which to draw a legitimate conclusion.

Nonetheless, you must start somewhere—and by recording every bet you make, you'll discover the truth about your racetrack betting. The most efficient way to do this is via computer, but even a handwritten ledger is far more than most players even attempt.

Let's look at what a computer can do for you. Do you fare better in races on the turf or on the dirt? Do you crush cheap claimers? Do your repeaters repeat? Do you win your $10 bets while losing your $50 plunges? How much success have you had playing the track's leading trainer in allowance races?

Most players don't know, which is one reason why so many don't improve their performance from one year to the next. But a computer can show exactly how, and what, you're doing. While many of the facts you'll learn are merely interesting, some nuggets may cause you to fundamentally alter your approach—and possibly increase your profits dramatically.

While many players use computers for handicapping and record-keeping in areas such as trainer statistics, few use them to analyze their bets. That's too bad, because how you bet—not merely how many winners you pick—will determine your success.

Until the advent of personal computers, keeping detailed bet records was difficult. Few players bothered with anything more complex than profit-and-loss totals. But now it's easy to track a dozen variables or more —and the sharp bettor will gain insights into his own betting that he never could with simple handwritten notebooks.

The key is data-base management software. I use a program called DBase II, but even more powerful ones are on the market. They all work in the same way: You enter bits of data, then ask the software to do certain tasks with the information. You needn't know how to write a program nor know much about a computer works. Any decent manual will show you how to set up a data base.

Depending on the capacity of your computer, you can be as creative as you want. I like to see everything about a play on a single line on the screen, so I limit what I enter to 80 spaces. When printed out, it looks like this:

Date	R	Horse	P	Drive	Train	MyOd	Odds	S	Bet	Coll	Fi	Class	LR
3/20	3	LadyL	3	Baker	Perez	*9-5	7-2	C	160	0	2&	T$16-20	1
3/20	4	AmylaseAm	7	Acker	Acker	*1	*9-5	C	300	870	1	CNW6	1

Both these horses raced on 3/20. Lady L, in the third race, was driven from post 3 by Baker and trained by Perez. I made her the favorite (*) at 9-5 on my own line and she went off at 7-2 in a race I rated C on my A-B-C scale. I bet $160 to win and collected zero when she finished second, beaten by the favorite (&) in a trot (T) for $16-20,000 claimers. She had finished first in her last race.

The next horse, Amylase Ambler, raced from post 7 in the fourth race. Trained and driven by Ackerman, the horse was 1-1 on my odds line. Fortunately, the fans let him get away at an overlaid 9-5 in this C race. I bet $300 to win and collected $870 when he did. The race was a conditioned claimer for non-winners of six races. He too had finished first in his last start.

Analyze whatever you please. Thoroughbred players may record distances, turf/dirt, workout patterns, or paddock notes. Greyhound bettors might have three possibilities for a Grade B bet—"B +" if the dog moved up from C, "B-" if the dog just dropped from A, or "B" if the dog remained in the same company. Some players may want to list morning-line odds, or comment briefly about the performance, or include place and show bets. The possibilities are endless.

Once you've created the data base you want, it takes about one minute per bet to enter the information. Since I usually bet about five races a day, it takes me less than half an hour a week to register all my bets.

If your data base is tiny, your information won't be worth much. After 25 bets, you can't tell a thing—but you don't want to wait two years before you have enough facts to draw conclusions, so haul out your old programs (but don't use any more than two years old; we're looking for current trends, not ancient history). If you don't have exact records, recreate your plays as best you can.

The fun comes after you've entered a long series of wagers, a minimum of 500. Start by printing a list of all your bets. You will immediately be struck by patterns. While you may have had some sense of them without any written records, it's fascinating to see every play listed in black and white.

Your next move is to print the totals—number of bets, wins and win percentage, money bet, money collected, and profit/loss total and percentage. This will give you a standard against which to measure your specific questions.

For example, let's say during a certain year your win-bet totals looked like this:

Bet:	$89,320
Coll:	$97,474
P/L:	+$8,154 (+9.1%)
Plays:	938
Wins:	264 (28.1%)

Now you can move on to simple queries:
1. What is my win percentage on favorites?
2. Print a list of my bets on horses ridden by Pincay.
3. What is my profit/loss on bets over $100?
4. How often did my allowance bets hit the board?

Even such basic questions as these may cause you to alter your methods. For example, you may find that you won 31% of your bets on Pincay, but the prices were so low that you showed a 40% flat-bet loss. Or you may discover that your profit/loss on your major bets was much different from your profit/loss on your small bets. Look further to see what the reasons might have been.

Sad news is just as useful as happy news—you can either correct the problem, or accept that you have no clue about (for instance) handicap races and then either pass them or play just a token amount. One year, for example,I disastrously overestimated the winning chances of a certain type of favorite and my big bets were virtually donations. By analyzing the printout, I was able to correct my error for the next meeting.

Your queries may get as detailed as you want:
1. Total amounts bet/collected for all bets on horses from post 1 in six-furlong sprints.
2. List all bets on Mike Mitchell dropdowns if I made the horse the favorite on my own line.
3. Total profits for turf races where my horse was switching jockeys and had finished unplaced last start.
4. List all bets of $50 or more I made in starter handicaps where the horse I bet went off at 3-1 or higher.

Be careful about drawing conclusions based on small sample sizes. Even with a data base of 1000 plays, you may have sub-groups that consist of only four bets (e.g., #3 above). You can't conclude much from such a sample. Still, glancing through even a short list on a screen is better than ignoring a fact altogether.

While recording information onto a computer won't necessarily make you into a winning player, it will certainly give you a realistic view of your ability.

Let's say, though, that not only don't you have a computer, but the whole idea of keeping detailed records bores you to tears. Then, at least, keep a summary of your daily activity, using a bookkeepers ledger or your own forms. A typical form:

Date	WB	WC	PB	PC	SB	SC	EB	EC	OB	OC	TB	TC	NP(L)
8/16	400	570	100	160	220	130	265	325	100	120	1085	1305	+220
17	150	–	50	70	200	280	250	610	50	–	700	960	+260

The "B" and "C" in most headings stand for bet and collected, while the first letters designate win, place, show, exactas, other exotics, and total. The final column represents net profit or loss. This player, for example, made $170 profit on win bets the first night (and $220 total) and lost $150 on win bets the second (though earning $260 for the evening).

I also register how my key horses did in each category (e.g., win keys for day = 4-1-1-0, exacta keys = 6-2-1-0, etc.) and I write a nightly overall comment. By keeping such notes, you'll discover which bets are most (and least) profitable for you. You'll have a true picture of your own skill —and you'll be able to chart your progress as a handicapper and bettor.

Record your expenses, which you should keep to a minimum. Go with a friend to share gas costs. Try to wangle an admission pass (at most tracks, owners and trainers receive extras), or at the very least use coupon books or other discounts. One enterprising player I knew used a color copier to make a facsimile of that season's parking sticker and blithely drove through the pass gate each night.

A sure way to reduce expenses—as well as keep your friends—is to *never lend or borrow money.* I figure that if a bank with a billion dollars in assets can't lend someone $500, I certainly can't either. By stating my policy to all, I never have to hear such nonsense as "But you lent Jimmy $100" or "I'll have it for you Tuesday."

Once your records have shown you to be a winner, your next decision is how much to play.

HOW MUCH TO BET

Some players use a simple strategy for bet sizing—however much money they've brought to the track that day is their bankroll. If they run out by the seventh race, so be it.

If you consider racetrack betting a business, this clearly won't do. A shoe store shouldn't run out of shoes, a bakery shouldn't run out of bread, and you shouldn't run out of cash.

Bet sizing is a complex matter. Among the considerations:
- Bankroll size
- How much you like the race (A-B-C)
- Amount of value offered
- Likelihood of that bet's winning
- Impact on the tote board
- Your emotional betting threshhold

While it's true that betting $5 a race probably won't finance a Beverly Hills mansion, overbetting is worse. Computer simulations and a formula known as gamblers ruin have shown that even a winning player who bets with an advantage on every wager may lose his entire stake if he overbets.

Exactly what the risk is depends on several factors—the size of your bankroll, the advantage per bet, and the amount wagered. For example, with a $10,000 bankroll and an average bet of $10 per race your chance of going bankrupt is virtually nil. But if you raise your bet to $500 to take a shot at making some big money, you dramatically increase your chances of tapping out.

We don't even want to think of what would happen if you're a losing player. Suffice it to say that if you bet sums that cause you to fall behind in the rent, you may soon find yourself in front of a gathering and saying, "My name is Joe. I am a compulsive gambler."

Most players lose. Such is the nature of the game. Then again, most players never read handicapping books, never keep statistics, never watch replays, and never take notes, either. Just because most people don't win doesn't mean *you* can't win.

To win, you have to cash enough tickets at sufficient prices to beat not only the other players, but the takeout as well. If you don't know your win percentage and average mutuel, it's tough to tell whether or not you can win.

Here are some possible winning combinations:

Win Bets
31% at average mutuel of $ 7.00 yields 8.5% profit
20% at average mutuel of $11.00 yields 10.0% profit

Place Bets
47% at average mutuel of $ 4.60 yields 8.1% profit
60% at average mutuel of $ 3.80 yields 14.0% profit

Show Bets
75% at average mutuel of $ 2.80 yields 5.0% profit
64% at average mutuel of $ 3.60 yields 15.2% profit

Assuming you have a 10% advantage on every bet and you bet $30 per race five times a night, your typical profit for an evening's work will be $15, which is less than you could have earned as an assistant bun boy at McDonald's. That does beat losing, however, which immediately puts you ahead of 95% of all players right off the top. And there is hope for much better ahead.

For if you continue to win and build your bankroll, you may within a couple of years start to be able to afford bets of $200 or more per race. It is not unusual for successful pros to bet $10,000 or more per week—and at a 10% advantage, that means profits of $1,000 and up weekly.

Divide your bankroll into several portions—one for win bets, another for place and show, and a third for quinellas, exactas, daily doubles, and pick 3's. Because bets such as trifectas, super bets (two exactas followed by a trifecta), pick 6's, and other exotic wagers demand large bankrolls to play to best advantage, skip these unless you don't mind betting thousands of dollars in a single week.

Even for an A play, *never risk more than 5% of your total bankroll in bets on a single race.* Let's say your betting capital is $5000, of which you set aside $2000 for win bets, $1000 for place and show, and $2000 for exactas (you can get by with lower place and show bankrolls because losing streaks are less frequent). Your maximum play for a race would be $250, though how much you'd risk in each category depends on the race.

Computer simulation programs make it possible to check on any money management strategy for thousands of mind bets. A typical simulation was reported by Dick Mitchell in *Thoroughbred Handicapping as an Investment*:

> A bettor hits 30% winners at a $7 average mutuel, an edge of 5%, and starts with a $1000 bankroll. When bets were limited to $20 or less, the player never tapped out. But when he raised his bet to $50 per play, he lost his entire bankroll 30% of the time.

A similar result was reported by William Quirin in *Winning At The Races*, which found the average profit per bet peaked with $20 bets and declined steadily as bets grew larger. However, the more you bet, the faster your bankroll will grow in good times. While you can easily blow a $1,000 bankroll by betting $100 a race even with a 10% advantage, big bets give you the chance for big scores—though a losing cycle will send your bankroll tumbling into a black hole. You must decide the risk you're willing to take.

The tradeoff between growth and safety is best addressed by a mathematical principle known as the *Kelly criterion.* It recommends bets based on your advantage per bet, as modified by the odds. The formula is:

Optimal Bet = Edge ÷ Odds

If, for example, you calculate that you have an 8% edge on an exacta that's returning $46 for $2 (22-1), your correct bet would be 0.36% of your capital. With a $2,000 bankroll, for example, your bet would be $7. To bet a 6-5 shot to win assuming you had a similar advantage, your bet would be 6.7% of your bankroll, or $134.

Kelly recommends a 6.7% play, but we said that no bet should be more than 5% of your bankroll. This brings up the problem with using Kelly as a betting system at racetracks—*your edge is always subjective, never objective.* You may believe you have a 25% edge on a particular race but it's possible you merely handicapped the race incorrectly; if you followed Kelly exactly, you might make a very large wager on what is really a bad play.

So in the bet charts in this book, rather than using the recommended Kelly betting strategy, we will use a fractional Kelly scheme based on reasonable real-world assumptions, rather than the hoped-for 50% or 60% theoretical edges we believe we have on certain plays.

Bet more than usual when your opinion is strong, less when it is weak. I use a ratio of $1 on a C race, $2 on a B, and $3 on an A. Experience will be your best guide as far as determining which races will yield you the greatest profits.

Your next standard for bet sizing is the amount of value on the race. If you make a horse 2-1, you wouldn't play unless the crowd lets him away at 3-1 or higher. If he's 7-2, bet more. If he's 4-1, bet still more.

Though two overlays seem to offer the same percentage value, bet more on the one at lower odds. This follows Kelly. Let's say, for example, that in one race a horse you make 2-1 is being let away at 3-1 and in another your 6-1 is being put up at 9-1. Assume that your records have shown you have a 10% edge in each situation. Your first bet would be 3.3% of bankroll (.10 ÷ 3), while your second would be 1.1% of bankroll (.10 ÷ 9).

The major reason to bet less on longer-odds horses is that losing streaks will run much longer. Taking this to an extreme, let's say a $2 exacta combination that fair value says should pay $250 is being put up on the board at $378. Nice—but even so, you expect that combination to win only once in 125 tries. It is no impossibility for that number to blow 327 times in a row. Because of that, keep your bets on high-odds combinations small.

Your next measure will be the impact on the tote board of your bet. No matter how small your wager, it will make some impression. Let's say that a horse you think deserves 32% of the place pool has only 27%. Before you act, calculate whether your proposed play would push the horse over the 32% limit (e.g., there's $2,000 in the place pool with $540 on your horse; a $150 bet would knock him into underlay-land).

The last consideration—but possibly the most important—is your emotional betting threshhold. A racing writer might tell you to think of money merely as "betting units," but if your bet chart says to bet $300 on this horse, that's cold cash. If you feel nervous betting that kind of money, scale your bets down to what feels comfortable.

Otherwise, if you lose some big bets, panic may set in. You might be tempted to chase after major losses by increasing your bets alarmingly, your judgment may suffer, and you could set yourself up for a terrible fall. *Nobody says your big bet has to win.*

It is always better to bet too little than too much. It may take you a little longer to accumulate a large sum, but that is far better than the opposite possibility.

In many races, you will find overlays in no pools. Even though you may loved the race in the morning, that means pass.

The optimal bet, we've seen, is your edge divided by the odds—with the caveat that your perceived edge in pari-mutuel racing is always subjective, which is why you must place a percentage-of-bankroll ceiling on what may seem like giant-edge bets. A number of how-to-win-a-trillion-in-a-week books, though, have recommended other betting schemes. None are as effective as the Kelly method, and a few are dangerous.

Take, for instance, the due-column betting system. The idea is to try to win a certain amount per race, or per day, then quit after you've reached your goal. If you try to make $20 a day, for instance, and your first horse is 2-1, you'd bet $10. If he loses, your new goal is $30, and if your next selection is 5-1 you'd bet $6.

Unfortunately for due-column betting, martingale (double-up) betting, and any other system that calls for you to increase your stakes as you lose, you never know when your next winner is coming from—or your next loser, either. Streaks come and go for no fathomable reason other than the vagaries of mathematics. You might win six straight bets, then lose the next twenty. Two examples from harness meets at Fairplex Park should suffice:

    1986—Favorites won 39%, but during one streak lost 22 straight

    1987—Favorites won 45.3% (222 of 490, one of the highest percentages ever for such
        a long meet), yet at one point lost 16 straight

It's true that for any particular day, a double-up or due-column method will probably yield a profit. It's also true that over a long period of time, you're going to encounter a losing streak. While merely annoyingly unpleasant with a conservative betting method, such a streak is fatal to a bet-raising scheme.

Every betting method must be measured by these standards:
- *If I'm winning, how fast will my profits accumulate?*
- *If I'm losing, what is the risk of a wipeout?*

Anyone can find a sequence where Betting System A will outperform Betting System B. Computer simulations, which can easily track 1000 random sequences given a particular win percentage and average payoff, have conclusively demonstrated the power of the Kelly method. (The results of some of these simulations can be found in Mitchell's books and in *Betting At The Racetrack* by William Ziemba and Donald Hausch.)

To make $600 a week at racetrack betting, assuming you have an overall 8% edge, you'll need to bet $1500 a day. Even if you stay away from high-risk plays such as non-partnership trifectas or pick 6's, that means you'd need a bankroll approaching $10,000. Part-time players, of course, won't need as much.

The bet-size recommendations in this book—for win, place, show, quinellas, exactas, and daily doubles—generally assume a $2,000 bankroll for each type of bet, but this can vary depending on how often you make a specific bet. At a track which offers nine races a day with just four exactas and a lone daily double, a 75-day meet would yield a maximum of 675 possible straight bets but only 300 exactas and 75 doubles. You need not maintain a large show-bet bankroll because you'll cash frequently; you also need not maintain a large daily double bankroll because you won't be betting very many of them.

Some players adjust their bankroll after every bet, which is probably a little much. But if you continue to make bets as if you have a $5,000 bankroll when you're down to your last $200, you're going to have a problem. And if you're betting as though you have a $5,000 bankroll when you've already run it up to $18,000, overly conservative betting may prove costly. I adjust my bet charts after every 200 wagers.

The amount of your bankroll should be the amount you could afford to lose without having to get credit-card advances to pay your rent. Keep it separate from your normal household budget. It may, or may not, reflect your previous 200-bet series of profits or losses. For example, let's say you began the year with a $7,000 racing bankroll, then ran it up to $23,000. Good—but maybe you have only $3,000 gambling money left because you've thrown away $20,000 in the stock market. Base your bet-sizing chart on $3,000 rather than $23,000.

When in doubt about whether to make a play—a certain pick 6 might require too large a bet, a horse has slightly too much money in the show pool to bet him there, you don't have an opinion on a maiden claimer, etc.—pass. There will always be other wagers, and other days.

WIN BETTING

You'll probably be making win bets every day, though not necessarily on your top choices.

Since you'll always seek the best bet for the odds, you never know what you're going to play until the public puts up the numbers. Unless a horse is at least 50% higher than your odds line (as close to post time as possible), don't play.

Note that if you make a horse 6-5 in an A race and he's only 7-5, don't play. If you make another horse a lukewarm 6-1 in a C and he's sent away at 10-1, play—even though he's only your fifth choice in a race you didn't like very much anyway. Never play odds-on horses unless you've made them 2-5 or less on your line and they go off at 4-5; such a play might come up twice a meeting. (Sometimes, you'll be stuck with an odds-on horse if the odds drop after you've bet.)

Don't play a horse to win unless you've made him 6-1 or below on your odds line. One reason for this is that as your odds assignments go up, the chance of your making a mistake increases; for example, if you made a horse 15-1 instead of 25-1 (a mere 2-point error out of 100 on the odds pie), you might bet 23-1 shots that are underlays rather than overlays. Second, once you get too far down the line and start betting fifth and sixth choices, you may wind up putting too much of your capital on horses you don't like very much.

Win Overlays	
Your Line	**Odds Required**
2-5 or below	4-5
1-2 or 3-5	1-1
4-5	6-5
1-1	3-2
6-5	9-5
7-5 or 3-2	2-1
8-5 or 9-5	5-2
2-1	3-1
5-2	7-2
3-1	9-2
7-2	5-1
4-1	6-1
9-2 or 5-1	7-1
6-1	9-1
7-1 or above	exactas only

Assuming your odds line is accurate, the 50% requirement theoretically insures at least a 22% edge on every bet (a 4-5 shot going off at 6-5 yields 22.2%, while a 9-2 shot going off at 7-1 yields 45.5%). But as you will no doubt sadly discover, underlays always outperform overlays—thus the 50% bonus demand. If your 1-1 overlays win just 42% of the time at a payoff of $5.00, you'll still maintain a 5% edge—enough to succeed. And, of course, sometimes your 1-1 shots will pay $5.40 or $6.00.

Once you've eliminated a horse by lining him out, don't bet him to win even if he winds up an overlay (e.g., you line a horse out but still make him 6-1 on your odds line and he goes off at 9-1; pass him). Restrict your bets to your contenders.

When betting overlays, beware the free-lunch factor. When you decide that a horse is an overlay, you're pitting your judgment against that of the public—and the fans are not all oafs. If you rate a horse 2-5 but the public makes him 7-2, you've probably overestimated the horse. Your overlays will usually come from lesser mistakes—the public has failed to recognize a crucial negative trainer change, overrated a pacer's recent suckalong fast mile, overlooked a dog's three-week layoff, etc. These errors cause the prices of the other entrants to drift upwards.

Some players don't like to bet an overlay because they feel the horse is cold—either he's not well meant, or he's gone off form since his last race. While it's true that occasionally you will bet on a 9-5 shot who should have been 1-1 but isn't because the horse is dead, my records show that long-term profits come from betting overlays indiscriminately, without trying to guess the stable's intentions. Horses win every day with not a single penny bet on them by anyone connected with the barn.

Since win pools are often twice the combined place-show pool, you can bet higher amounts to win than in the secondary slots. However, don't bet so much that the toteboard vibrates after your bet. To determine your maximum bet, record the final pools for two typical days at your track —one midweek and one weekend. Using a calculator, you'll learn how much of a bet will affect the final odds. You can then devise a pair of bet charts using amounts that won't eliminate your edge.

Let's say, for example, that the typical Wednesday win pool totals $14,000 with a 17% takeout. These would be the amounts bet on several horses:

1-1	$5,810
2-1	$3,873
4-1	$2,324
10-1	$1,056

A mere $200 win bet on the 10-1 shot would slash its odds to 8-1, underlay country—so such a bet would be too high even with a $500,000 bankroll. Your maximum bet, if you made the horse 6-1 on your line (and thus needed 9-1 to play), would be $115.

On Saturday, with $25,000 in the win pool, these would be the amounts:

1-1	$10,375
2-1	$ 6,917
4-1	$ 4,150
10-1	$ 1,886

A $200 bet on the 10-1 shot would still leave this horse at 9-1 ($25,200 × .83 − 2086 ÷ 2086 = $9.02 to 1).

While you can make major plays on a Sunday at Santa Anita where $5 million may be bet, you can't overbet on a Tuesday at Pocono Downs. The smaller the track, the more important it is to make up the two bet charts.

On the next page is a chart listing win bets assuming a $2,000 win-bet capital—not $2,000 total capital. It assumes this is the amount you

WIN BET CHART
(Capital = $2000)

	4/5	1	6/5	7/5	3/2	8/5	9/5	2	5/2	3	7/2	4	9/2	5	6	7	8	9	10
1/5	125																		
2/5	100																		
1/2		80	83	85															
3/5		60	66	71	80														
4/5			50	57	66	75													
1					40	50	55	60											
6/5							35	40											
7/5								30	32	33	34								
3/2								26	27	29	31	33							
8/5									24	26	28	30	31						
9/5									21	23	25	27	28	29					
2										20	22	25	26	28					
5/2										17	20	22	24						
3														13	16	16	17		
7/2															12	13	14	15	
4															10	11	12	13	14
9/2																8	10	11	12
5																5	7	8	10
6																		6	8

The numbers on the left refer to your own odds line. The numbers at the top refer to the tote odds. If, for example, you make a horse 6-5 and the crowd lists him at 9-5, you would bet $35. If they send him away at 2-1, raise your bet to $40.

If an overlay is not listed on the chart (e.g., your 3-5 shot goes off at 8-5), play the highest listed number (in this case, $80).

The numbers assume the race is average (rated B on an A-B-C scale of interest in a race). If you rate a race as C, bet less; if A, bet more. If your capital fund is more or less than $2000, adjust these figures accordingly.

have to risk on *win bets only*. Looking over my own betting records, I find that about 40% of my betting action is to win. If your betting is similar, then the chart can be used as is if your total betting capital is $5,000 (since 40% of $5,000 is $2,000). If your capital is greater or lesser, adjust these amounts by the appropriate percentage (though your high-end bets are limited by possible tote-board influence).

The numbers were derived by assuming that instead of your odds line's being accurate, it is only accurate to the point where you will earn a 6% edge on minimum overlays, 8% on overlays of one extra column, 10% on overlays of two extra columns, and 12% on overlays of three extra columns, and then using half the Kelly recommendation rather than full Kelly for security. Thus, if it is in error, it errs on the side of safety.

In 1000 computer trials of 700 races reported by Ziemba and Hausch in their book *Betting at the Racetrack*, the .5 Kelly betting scheme assuming a 10% overall edge yielded a profit 82.7% of the time and recorded an excellent $1,928 median bankroll off a $1,000 starting billfold—not quite as high as the full Kelly, but the bankroll dropped below $500 only 3.3% of the time compared with 13.5% for full Kelly.

Note that the largest bets are those with the greatest chance of winning—the horses you list at even money and below. Although your bets also increase as the edge becomes larger, *the key is the frequency of wins* —not the size of the advantage.

The small bets in the chart (e.g., $6 to win on a horse you rate 6-1 who goes off at 9-1) won't bring you a million dollars in a week. However, their conservatism makes it unlikely that you will go bust. And, assuming your handicapping improves with experience, your capital will grow larger which will enable you to increase your bets.

Even though the bet sizes may seem tiny, your handle for a particular night could still be large. On a single race, for instance, you might bet $40 to win, another $40 in the exacta, $50 to place, $100 to show, and $20 in the daily double. Make six such bets a day and you've put $1500 through the windows. And if your long-term records show you to be a player who wins at a much larger advantage than our estimate of 8% to 10%, you can safely bet higher amounts.

At times, two contenders will be listed at least 50% above your odds line. Recently I checked the results of 12 meetings which yielded 420 races in which I had two or more horses above the 50% overlay mark (of which nearly all had only two horses above the line). Playing both (or all) overlays would have resulted in net profits for 9 of those 12 meetings. Conclusion: If two horses are overlaid, bet them both, a la Speedy Sam and Wily Willie.

When you bet more than one horse in a race, you are guaranteed at least one losing bet—so you must subtract that losing wager before considering whether the bet is still an overlay. If one horse is 2-1 and another is 5-2, even if both are overlays you'll wind up with less than even money for your action. That's why I insist on at least 3-1 for any horse that's part of a two-horse overlay.

Two-Horse Overlays

Your Line	Odds Required If 2 Overlays
3-2 or below	3-1
8-5 or 9-5	7-2
2-1	4-1
5-2	9-2
3-1 or 7-2	6-1
4-1	7-1
9-2	8-1
5-1	9-1
6-1	10-1

If only one horse meets these more difficult overlay requirements, then play that horse only. For example, let's say a 6-5 shot on your line is listed at 2-1 and a 4-1 shot is listed at 8-1. Skip the 2-1 shot and play the 8-1 shot only.

Some players prefer to *dutch*, using a formula that enables them to play two horses in a race and collect the same profit no matter which one wins. Dutching helps prevent long losing streaks, since generally when you bet only one overlay you'll be passing the one at low odds, which is more likely to win. However, you also are laying out a lot more money to collect small profits—and often, both overlays lose.

To determine the amount to bet on each contestant when you dutch, check the odds-percentage table and bet the horses in that ratio. In the above case, the numbers are 33% for a 2-1 shot and 11% for an 8-1, so you'd bet three times as much on the lower-priced horse (for example, $33 on the 2-1 shot and $11 on the 8-1 shot, so no matter which horse wins, you'd get back $99 and show a $55 profit). To bet three horses whose odds are 3-1, 5-1, and 8-1, you'd bet in the ratio of $25, $16, and $11, respectively. The best time to dutch is when you hate the favorite or second choice. Since the odds of the horses you'll be dutching may equal 50% or even as much as 60%, you can't afford too many errors when you dutch —but when you're right, you'll sometimes feel almost guilty about stealing the few dollars profit.

	Horse	Your Odds	Tote Odds	Tote – L	Bet Size
Race I	A	2-1	4-1	3-1	20
	B	6-1	12-1	11-1	8
Race II	C	7-2	6-1	5-1	12
	D	4-1	11-1	10-1	14
Race III	E	6-5	5-2	3-2	-
	F	5-1	9-1	8-1	7
Race IV	G	3-2	7-2	5-2	27
	H	6-1	9-1	8-1	-
Race V	I	5-2	4-1	3-1	-
	J	5-1	7-1	6-1	-
Race VI	K	5-2	9-2	5-2	-
	L	4-1	10-1	8-1	12
	M	5-1	8-1	6-1	-

These are not really optimal amounts for long-term bankroll growth, however, because they don't take into account the amount of overlay for either the group as a whole or for any of the individual horses. An alternative, well thought-out method for calculating how best to bet group overlays is contained in a report, *Bankroll Control* by Michael Pascual, though it may prove a bit technical unless you're a mathematics professor.

Because odds constantly change at the track, sometimes we have to compromise, giving up an optimal betting strategy for a not-so-perfect but more practical method that works in the frantic moments just before post time. Instead of dutching, if two horses meet the tougher double-overlay qualifying standard then *play them both according to the amount on the bet chart after deducting the losing bet* (or bets, if more than two horses are overlaid) as the chart indicates.

The chart on page 52 gives examples of the most common dutching situations. Note that the third column of figures (Tote – L) is determined by subtracting one losing bet from the tote odds if there are two overlays, or two losing bets if there are three overlays (as in Race VI). The Tote – L column is the one to check on your bet chart; if the horse still qualifies as an overlay in that column (compared with your line in the first column), then bet the amounts in the bet chart. Note that any combinations are possible—sometimes betting only the longer-priced horse, sometimes just the shorter, sometimes both in varying amounts, sometimes neither.

What we think is really a 45% edge on a particular play may actually prove to be only 6% when we total our wins and losses for the season—so don't be misled by bet charts that claim you may safely bet much larger percentages of your bankroll, or you'll be overbetting dangerously. Play conservatively and watch your money grow in stages.

PLACE AND SHOW BETTING

The public underbets favorites and low-odds horses even more to place and show than to win—and by monitoring the pools, we can occasionally find overlays. Because many back-up bettors are casual fans, the crowd generally far overbets longshots in these slots, leading to overlays on the favorites.

It takes no special genius to figure that if Horse A has 50% of the win pool but only 25% of the place pool and 25% of the show pool, he may be overbet to win or underbet in the other slots. If it's the latter, you may have a play.

Before getting to the fun part—how to make money betting place and show—let's look at some of the disadvantages:
   • *You never make a score.* Place and show betting is grinding. While you could make $7,000 on a $50 exacta bet, even a $500 show bet may barely get you back pocket change.
   • *You must hit a high percentage.* If your show payoffs average $2.40 and you hit 80%, you lose.
   • *You are buried by takeout and breakage.* The latter alone might reduce a payoff from $2.39 to $2.20.
   • *If you bet big at a small track, you wind up betting against yourself.* As little as a $50 show bet may materially affect your payoff at some tracks.
   • *You don't know for sure what your payoff will be,* since it will depend on what other horse or horses come in with your selection.
   • *You can't see the toteboard* from the betting lines at some tracks.

If you must get on line early for other bets, you won't have the latest, best information about the backup slots.

 • *You will always pick more winners* than horses that finish second or third, so that much of the time you would have won more money by betting the horse to win.

So why bet place or show?

To save a bet? Nope. A bet cannot be protected. It either wins or loses. Betting a horse to place or show is a completely separate play.

To continue a parlay? No again. Once you win a bet, it's not "the track's money"—it's your money. If you don't ordinarily bet $137 to show on a horse, don't do it just because you won a bet the previous half hour.

To play a horse you think may not be good enough to win but should hit the board? Why bet a horse you don't think is capable of winning the race? Why not, instead, bet the horse you do think can win?

There is only one reason to bet place and/or show—if a horse (or an entry) is an overlay.

Place and show betting had been largely forgotten by racing authors until the publication of *Beat The Racetrack* by William Ziemba and Donald Hausch in 1984. The authors offered mathematical formulas that, they wrote, would detect place and show overlays. They called their method the Dr Z System. Their idea was simple: Since it's been shown that the win pool is efficient (4-5 shots win more than 1-1 shots, which win more than 6-5 shots, etc.), why not use that win-end public efficiency to discover underbet place and show horses?

The problem, however, was that no one had researched whether the place and show pools *by themselves* were efficient. Take two horses, Seconditis and Classy Lameo. Seconditis hates to win but his joy in life is to finish close to the leaders. Classy Lameo hasn't raced in eight months but is dropping three classes. Classy Lameo is the favorite in the win pool but Seconditis is the favorite in the show pool. Is this market inefficiency, or has the public correctly figured that if Classy Lameo doesn't win, he won't hit the board?

In addition, the authors made serious miscalculations in their follow-up book, *Betting At The Racetrack*, drastically overestimating the correct in-the-money percentages for various ranges of post-time odds.They used an algorithm, known as the Harville formulas, for their reckoning of how often a horse in a certain win odds range should hit the board. Unfortunately, the formulas are wrong.

To look more closely at in-the-money percentages for odds-on horses —the most frequent Dr. Z System bets—I checked 1000 odds-on favorites at thoroughbred, quarterhorse, and harness tracks across the U.S. and Canada. To insure randomness, I took a stack of *Daily Racing Forms* from different times of the year and noted the finishing position of every odds-on finisher in all charts. (I also checked on the relationship between odds-on success and field size, but there was no significant difference between large and small fields.) Here were the results:

Odds To $1	S	1	2	3	W%	P% DrZ	Diff	S% DrZ	Diff
Under $.20	7	6	1	0	.86	all (98.0)	+2.0	all (98.5)	+1.5
$.20- $.39	80	67	5	3	.84	90.0 (95.8)	−5.8	93.7 (98.0)	−4.3
$.40- $.49	83	53	13	6	.64	79.5 (89.2)	−9.7	86.7 (97.3)	−10.6
$.50- $.59	93	55	14	15	.59	74.2 (85.4)	−11.2	90.3 (95.5)	−5.2
$.60- $.79	304	162	63	32	.53	74.0 (81.8)	−7.8	84.5 (93.8)	−9.3
$.80- $.99	433	206	109	46	.48	72.7 (76.2)	−3.5	83.4 (90.6)	−7.2
Totals	1000	549	205	102	.55	75.4		85.6	

Excluding the category of "under $.20" where the sample size was miniscule, every odds category was greatly overestimated in the Ziemba-Hausch book. The differences ranged from 3.5% short in 4-5 shots to place (Dr Z predicted 76.2%, actually 72.7%) to 11.2% among 1-2 shots to place (Dr Z predicted 85.4%, actually 74.2%). While the survey percentages would no doubt change somewhat with a larger sample size (e.g., 2-5 shots would doubtlessly hit the board more often than 1-2 shots), the consistency of the discrepancies throughout the odds ranges calls into question the authors' conclusions.

Still, there seems to be some evidence that low-odds horses may be underbet to place and show. Samplings of extremely heavy post-time favorites (1-2 and below), for example, usually show a small loss to a win but just about break even to place and show. And, with many serious players foregoing place and show betting, a greater percentage of the backup pools comes from casual fans, who notoriously overbet longshots at an even more severe clip than they do on the win end.

Before going on to our charts, let's look for a moment at the Ziemba-Hausch formulas for place and show overlays. Explaining how they were arrived at would tax anyone not related to Albert Einstein. These formulas assume a 17.1% takeout:

Place

$0.319 + 0.559 \dfrac{Wi \div W}{Pi \div P}$

Show

$0.543 + 0.369 \dfrac{Wi \div W}{Si \div S}$

$Wi \div W$, $Pi \div P$, and $Si \div S$ represent the ratios between the individual horse's bet in a particular pool (win, place, show) vs. the total bet in those pools. Take this example:

There is $1000 in the win pool, of which $500 has been bet on Tacoma Slew, so $Wi \div W$ equals 0.5. There is $200 in the place pool, of which the horse has only $60, so $Pi \div P$ equals 0.3. Therefore, the total would equal 0.319 + 0.559 (0.5 ÷ 0.3) or 1.25. Anything over 1.00 is an overlay, though Ziemba-Hausch require at least 1.14 to play.

By some clever mathematics, the authors conclude that there's no reason to concern yourself with how much money certain other horses have attracted in the place or show pools even though we all know that if our overlay comes in with the top two choices it's going to pay a heckuva lot less than if he comes in with the two longest shots on the board.

These calculations are a bit involved and require a miniature computer to operate at the racetrack—and there is a real question as to whether your results would equal those claimed by the system creators. But there is an alternative method that simplifies the work immensely, eliminates the need for an expensive computer program or the use of complicated formulas, and points to overlays with great accuracy. Just *use your own odds line and the accompanying chart*. The numbers assume a 17% takeout.

The numbers—the maximum percentage of the pool that can be bet on a horse in one of the backup slots and still yield a respectable overlay—were obtained by taking the percentage of the pool that puts a horse at a certain price (e.g., a 6-5 shot has 37.73% of the win pool), then dividing that percentage by 154 for place overlays and 173 for show overlays. (These divisors came from the Ziemba-Hausch toteboard guidelines which claim an 18% theoretical edge using them strictly from the board, though this number appears to come from fantasyland due to the false optimism of the inaccurate Harville formulas.)

Using your own win odds line simplifies calculations. Let's say you make a certain horse 6-5 on your line. You can bet him to place if he has 24.50% of the place pool or less; to show, the maximum is 21.81%. As close to post time as possible, simply check the percentage of the appropriate pool bet on the horse. Often you can eyeball it. Other times you'll need a calculator. An example for this 6-5 shot:

Place-Show Maximum Percentages

Your Odds	Place	Show
1-9	48.55	43.22
1-5	44.92	39.98
2-5	38.50	34.27
1-2	35.93	31.98
3-5	33.69	29.98
4-5	29.94	26.65
1-1	26.95	23.99
6-5	24.50	21.81
7-5	22.45	19.99
3-2	21.56	19.19
8-5	20.73	18.45
9-5	19.25	17.13
2-1	17.97	15.99
5-2	15.40	13.71
3-1	13.47	11.99
7-2	11.97	10.66
4-1	10.78	9.59
9-2 +	no play	no play

Place: $974 of $2975
Show: $211 of $1195

When looking for place and show overlays, ignore the win pool—just use your own odds line of 6-5. A quick glance shows that this horse has about one-third of the place pool, obviously far exceeding the 24.50% place maximum, so you needn't do any computations (the exact number is 974 ÷ 2975 = 32.7%). The show number looks close, though, so you press a couple of buttons on your calculator (211 ÷ 1195 = 17.6%) and discover the horse is playable to show. To get the amount to bet:
1. $1195 × .2181 = $260.62, rounded to $260
2. $260 − $211 (the amount already bet) = $49

You can bet $49 to show on your 6-5 shot. This amount is a trifle conservative, since your $49 bet would actually leave him with only 20.9% of the new pool (since the total pool would now rise to $1244). But this is a fast, practical way to calculate your optimal place/show maximum wagers.

A serious drawback to place and show betting is that since these pools are far smaller than win or exacta pools, a few big bettors—or even one —may eliminate an overlay after you've bet. For example, the place pool at a medium-sized track on a Tuesday is $4,000 with one minute to go. The favorite, which you rated at 3-5, has $1,200 on him. The chart tells you that this horse can be bet up to 33.69% of the place pool—$1,347— and remain an overlay. You bet. Except for one problem—15 seconds after you bet, somebody bets $300 to place on the big favorite, converting your fat overlay into a skinny, useless underlay.

There's nothing we can do about this. Even if you bet in the final few seconds, somebody at the next window may be destroying your overlay. While this is always a danger no matter whether you're betting the daily double or a quinella, small place and show pools are especially vulnerable to a late hit.

Still, the charts give us the best chance to make money in the backup slots. The numbers are maximums. For example, a horse you make 7-2 is playable with 22% of the place pool but not with 23%(though he still might be bettable to show, if he has 19.99% of the show pool or less).

Horses you list at 9-2 or higher will rarely be overlays to place or show. Most of your place and show bets will come from your top choices, often those you list at odds-on.

Place and show bets have nothing to do with whether the horse is an overlay in the win pool. Let's say a horse you make 9-5 is listed at 9-5 on the board, no value. However, he has only 15% of the show pool. As long as he's not a win-or-out type, bet him to show. Occasionally, you'll bet one horse to win and another to show.

Since losing streaks to place or show are usually not severe, you can safely bet a larger percentage of your bankroll on a race in the backup slots. Exactly how much to bet, however, is trickier. You can use the Kelly criterion, edge divided by odds—but only after you've determined what your average place and show odds are for each tick on your win-odds chart.

Take, for instance, horses you make 4-5 on your odds line that you bet to place because they're overlaid to place. What is their average payoff? How frequently do they hit the board? If they average $3.03 to place and finish in the top two 70% of the time, you'd have a 6% edge. Then, using Kelly, you'd get .06 ÷ .515 so that you could bet up to 11.6% of your place bankroll on these horses, or 5.8% using the recommended half-Kelly. Until you've studied the performances of each odds group, you can only guess at the correct bet sizes—though they surely will be higher than your win bets.

Without having done the study of your own bets suggested in the previous paragraph, you might estimate your bet size from the chart. It assumes a $2000 place bankroll and a $2000 show bankroll, with a minimum overlay and a bet that will not cause the horse to become an underlay.

Place-Show Bet Chart (Capital = $2000)		
Your Odds	**Place**	**Show**
1-9	450	600
1-5	225	300
2-5	150	225
1-2	120	160
3-5	90	120
4-5	75	100
1-1	60	80
6-5	50	66
7-5	45	60
3-2	39	52
8-5	36	48
9-5	31	42
2-1	30	40
5-2	25	34
3-1	19	26
7-2	18	24
4-1	15	20
9-2 +	no play	no play

These approximations came from the win betting table and assume that you can bet 150% of a win bet to place and 200% of a win bet to show because of the extra security available. With higher bankrolls, you can safely bet more.

However, large bets may eliminate your edge. So before making a play, figure the impact on the place or show total. For instance, the place pool totals $2000 and there is only $720 to place on a horse you list at 2-5, less than the 38.5% maximum that would take him out of range. However, if you bet $100 to place on him, that tips him over the edge.

To bet place or show, you must bet virtually at post time—and at many tracks, you can't view the shifting place and show totals from some betting lines. Try to bet from a spot where you can check the board and still play as late as possible, or enlist a partner who'll dash in and give you the ratios as you wait on line. At many race books and off-track betting parlors, however, you won't be able to see place and show pools at all; *if you can't see the pools, don't play.*

Although you should check the place and show pools in every race, pay particular attention when you make a horse 1-2 or below on your odds line. Usually, the public makes such a horse too short to play to win—but often you'll find value to place or show.

If your line is inaccurate, your win errors will be compounded to place and show. If, for example, you make a horse 4-5 when he should really be closer to 8-5, your mistakes will haunt you in the place and show slots as well. (Of course, if your line is consistently far off, you're not going to win anyway.) But if your line is accurate, and you avoid win-or-out types, the use of the conservative charts above will land you on solid backup slot overlays.

Totalling my own place and show plays for nine harness meetings from 1985-87 (382 place bets and 617 show bets with a total handle of nearly $200,000), both slots were profitable, though the net was less than 5% for each position. While this is certainly not as spectacular as the profits available from playing pick 6's, for example, place and show bankroll swings are minimal because of the high frequency of cashing. In not a single meeting, for example, did the final tallies to show lose more than 10% or win more than 10%.

When two horses are combined on a strong entry that looks as if it could finish 1-2 or 1-3, you may get gigantic place or show prices (8-5 to place on an even-money entry, for example). Therefore, you can increase the maximum permitted pool percentage to place or show by a certain amount, depending upon your odds. Ziemba and Hausch recommend that you take their formulas and add these fractions:

Place entry: Add $0.867 \text{ Wi} \div \text{W} - 0.857 \text{ Pi} \div \text{P}$
Show entry: Add $0.842 \text{ Wi} \div \text{W} - 0.810 \text{ Si} \div \text{S}$

When you are considering betting an entry to place or show, use the coupled-entry chart. It was developed from the Ziemba-Hausch suggestions.

Coupled-Entry Maximum Percentages

Your Odds	Place	Show
1-9	58.09	53.45
1-5	53.09	48.73
2-5	44.50	40.70
1-2	41.15	37.58
3-5	38.28	34.90
4-5	33.56	30.54
1-1	29.89	27.14
6-5	26.93	24.41
7-5	24.49	22.17
3-2	23.43	21.20
8-5	22.46	20.31
9-5	20.76	18.72
2-1	19.27	17.38
5-2	16.35	14.73
3-1	14.20	12.76
7-2	12.55	11.27
4-1	11.25	10.18
9-2 +	no play	no play

Usually, you'll find three or four backup bets per day. Although the requirements for a show bet are stiffer, you'll probably find twice as many show as place bets.

On rare occasions, the track suffers a minus pool, usually in the show slot. This occurs when so much is bet on one horse, or an entry, that no money is left to pay even the $2.10 minimum. If Stone Cinch has $21,000 of a $25,000 show pool, all the top three finishers will pay $2.10 if Cinch hits the board even if the other two in-the-money finishers are longshots that have only $50 each bet on them to show:

1. $25,000 − 17% takeout of $4250 .... $20,750
2. Amount bet on winners $21,100
3. Dividend to 1-2-3 finishers .... $ 0
4. Amount due winning ticket-holders $22,050
5. Minus pool ($22,050 − $20,750) .... $ 1,300

Since you must hit 95% winners merely to break even, minus-pool $2.10 sure things don't offer value. Once in awhile the following will occur:

> A six-horse race looks to be between a powerful two-horse entry and its only rival. You make the entry 2-5 and the second choice 3-1, with everyone else long. According to our chart, you can bet to show on a 3-1 shot if it has 11.99% or less of the show pool. You check the board and the 3-1 shot has only 8% to show. Good so far. But the entry has 78% of the show pool. If either half of the entry hits the board, your 3-1 shot will return only $2.10. Pass.

From time to time you'll hear about amazing payoffs to show because some plunger shoveled $100,000 through the windows on a seeming lock, only to see it finish up the track. But generally, avoid any race in which a minus pool seems imminent—you'll get no value on anyone in the race.

The advent of parlay betting in New York in 1988—which may spread to other tracks—has given us more potential profit in the place and show holes. Parlay players' winnings are automatically carried over to their next selections. Players are not permitted to cancel these carried-over bets. So occasionally, some no-account longshot will be far overbet to place or show, particularly in one of the late races on the card. That makes wagering on the legitimate favorites very attractive. So if you are at a track which allows parlays—don't bet these idiotic parlays yourself, of course—watch the place and show pools especially carefully.

Your place and show bets probably won't be your leading contributor to a profitable year. Still, if you can pick up a few additional dollars by catching backup overlays, it certainly won't hurt your profit-and-loss statement. And since your place and show bets will come in more often than your win or exacta plays, you'll get to visit the cashier more often. At the very least, that's a psychological plus in a game where how you feel affects how you play.

EXACTAS AND QUINELLAS

Exactas (picking the one-two finishers in order) and quinellas (picking them in either order) have taken over the racing game. It isn't unusual for the exotic handle for a race to total twice that of the win, place and show pools combined.

Fans love them. So do politicians. In most states, the exacta/quinella takeout exceeds the tax on straight wagers. At California harness tracks, for example, the takeout is 16.33% on straight bets and 24.08% on exotics. The pols have figured, correctly, that nobody collecting a $60 payoff would complain about a few missing dollars.

Let's first discuss the exacta (also called exactor or perfecta). Despite the excessive grab, it has become a key element in the professional bettor's arsenal. Values abound because uninformed bettors throw away so much money in fruitless attempts at a giant payoff.

Here's the downside of exacta betting:
  • *Confiscatory takeout.* It's tough enough beating a 15% take. It's that much harder beating a 20% or 25% slice.
  • *Limited maximum bets.* Even though far more money is usually bet in exactas than to win, it takes less money to move a number. In a 10-horse field with a $30,000 win pool and $50,000 exacta pool, $3,000 is bet on the average horse to win but only $555 on the typical exacta combo. Some longshot combos have just a handful of tickets.
  • *Higher required bankroll.* Even if the minimum bet is $2—and at some tracks, it's $3 or $5—you need a fat bankroll because of losing

streaks. You will always cash more win bets than exacta bets. And since it's no big deal to lose 20 straight win bets, we don't want to speculate on how many exactas in a row you can lose.

• *Missing final odds.* Since TV monitors may show a combination for 20 seconds, you may not be able to see the possible payoffs with your choice in the last few minutes of betting. Just when you think you've buried a $90 exacta, up on the board it goes at a lousy $58.

• *Psychological horrors.* Foremost of these is seeing your 15-1 key horse cruise home by four without the correct place horse. Or perhaps you invest $90 in the exacta and get back only $27, which gives you the thrill of both winning and losing in a single transaction.

• *The integrity factor.* Since half the money in exactas has the favorite either first or second, some jockeys and drivers have discovered there's easy money to be made by pulling the favorite, then loading up on the other contenders.

• *The IRS grab.* If by some miracle you do manage to hit a $734 number for your $2 wager, you will have to fill out tax forms. And if you hit a $1000 combo, 20% will immediately be withheld from your payoff. While it's possible that some or all of this might be refunded one year later, don't count on it.

Enough of this bad news. Let's look on the bright side.

Many fans play the exacta on hope. They bet birthdays, phone numbers, or sequences such as 1-2 or 7-11; they think the exacta is a lottery. Millions of these free dollars, not available to nearly the same extent in the win pool, help increase potential profits.

Other players have entirely the wrong approach and waste untold zillions more on such wasted moves as baseballing four horses or wheeling and back-wheeling their key horse with everything that moves. These fans seldom check a TV monitor and have no clue whether they will even make any money with their dozen combinations. Fortunately for us, just about none of them keep records, or else they would switch tactics.

Next advantage comes from those TV monitors. While some tracks flash all the exacta probables on the toteboard for everyone to see, at many others some effort is required to keep up to the minute—you've got to stand elbow to elbow amidst jostling gamblers, copying every number onto a pad. The typical fan either checks only a few combos, or bypasses the screens entirely on the way to plunk his dough on a three-horse box.

There is one reason, and one reason only, to make a bet. Does it offer value? This is just as true for exactas as it is for win, place, or show bets.

The questions, then, are these:
1. *What is the chance of a combination's finishing 1-2?*
2. *What is the payoff?*
3. *Is that price an overlay?*

You must make two calculations. First, what is the chance that a certain horse will win? Second, assuming the first horse wins, what is the chance that the other horse will run second?

Take the exacta of Fetlock and Pastern. You give Fetlock a 40% chance to win the race and Pastern 20%. Let's calculate a fair exacta payoff.

Out of a 100% round-book line, you've assigned Fetlock 40%. The rest of the field has 60%, of which Pastern has 20%, or one-third of the remainder. Thus the chance of this combination's finishing 1-2 is .40 $\times (.20 \div .60)$, or 13.3 chances in 100. Checking our friendly odds-percentage table (or calculating $1 \div .133 - 1$), we find this equals about 6.5 to 1. For a $2 bet, anything below $15 for this number is an underlay. Since we demand at least a 50% overlay for all bets, we need $22 ($6.5 \times 1.5 \times 2 + 2$ = $21.50, bumped to $22).

The computer-generated charts on the next three pages show the required price (for $2, $3, or $5 exacta minimums) for every possible combination assuming you use your own line and demand a 50% overlay bonus.

Just as with win betting, add the points assigned to each horse on a stable entry to determine the overall odds to use for the entry in the exacta, with one exception—if your jurisdiction permits entries to be split in the exacta pool. At some Canadian tracks, you can bet a 1-1 exacta. If so, then consider 1 and 1A to be separate entities when figuring your exactas.

A flaw in our exacta betting plan is that some horses—hanging, seconditis types—love to finish second but hate to win. And other horses —such as win-or-break trotters—are often nowhere if they don't finish first. So before relying on the chart for your exacta play for a particular race, make sure that neither type is a factor in the race (if it's a win-or-nowhere type, however, you can record the combos with him on top).

Things move fast in exacta pools. Keeping up with the ever-changing exacta odds requires concentration and a quick pencil. You will need a set of lined sheets (both a blank and a filled-in sample appear later in

$2 Exacta Overlay Prices

	1/5	2/5	1/2	3/5	4/5	1	6/5	7/5	3/2	8/5	9/5	2	5/2	3	7/2	4	9/2	5	6	7	8	9	10	11	12	15	20	25	30	50	100
1/9																							4	4	4	5	6	7	9	15	31
1/5																			4	4	5	5	6	7	7	9	12	15	18	31	61
2/5														4	5	5	6	7	8	9	10	11	13	15	16	20	26	32	38	62	122
1/2													5	5	6	7	8	8	10	11	12	14	16	17	18	23	31	38	46	77	152
3/5											5	5	6	7	8	8	9	10	12	14	16	17	19	22	24	28	37	46	55	91	181
4/5								5	5	6	6	7	8	9	10	11	13	14	16	18	21	23	26	28	31	38	50	63	75	123	242
1							6	7	7	7	8	8	10	11	13	14	16	17	20	23	26	29	32	35	38	47	62	77	92	152	302
6/5						7	7	8	8	9	10	10	12	14	16	17	19	21	25	28	32	35	39	43	46	57	75	93	111	183	363
7/5					8	8	9	10	10	11	11	12	14	16	18	20	23	25	29	33	37	41	46	50	54	67	88	109	130	214	
3/2					8	8	9	10	11	11	12	13	15	17	20	22	24	26	31	35	40	44	49	53	58	71	94	116	139	229	
8/5					8	9	10	11	11	12	13	14	16	18	21	23	26	28	33	38	43	47	52	57	62	76	100	124	148	244	
9/5				8	9	10	11	13	13	13	15	16	18	21	24	26	29	32	37	43	48	53	59	64	70	86	113	140	167	275	
2				9	10	11	13	14	14	15	16	17	20	23	26	29	32	35	41	47	53	59	65	71	77	95	125	155	185	305	
5/2				11	11	13	14	16	17	18	19	20	22	26	29	33	37	41	44	52	59	67	74	82	89	97	119	157	194	232	
3			12	13	14	16	17	19	21	22	23	25	26	31	35	40	44	49	53	62	71	80	89	98	107	116	143	188	233	278	
7/2			14	15	16	18	20	23	25	26	27	29	31	36	41	47	52	57	62	73	83	94	104	115	125	136	167	220	272	324	
4				16	17	18	21	23	26	28	29	31	33	35	41	47	53	59	65	71	83	95	107	119	131	143	155	191	251	311	
9/2				18	20	21	24	26	29	32	33	35	37	40	47	53	60	67	74	80	94	107	121	134	148	161	175	215	283		
5				20	22	23	26	28	32	35	37	38	41	44	47	59	67	74	82	89	104	119	134	149	164	179	194	239	314		
6	21	25	26	28	32	35	39	43	44	46	50	53	62	71	80	89	98	107	125	143	161	179	197	215	233	287					
7	25	29	31	33	37	41	46	50	52	54	58	62	73	83	94	104	115	125	146	167	188	209	230	251	272	335					
8	28	33	35	38	43	47	52	57	59	62	67	71	83	95	107	119	131	143	167	191	215	239	263	287	311						
9	32	37	40	43	48	53	59	64	67	70	75	80	94	107	121	134	148	161	188	215	242	269	296	323							
10	32/35	41	44	47	53	59	65	71	74	77	83	89	104	119	134	149	164	179	209	239	269	299	329								
11	35/39	46	49	52	59	65	72	79	82	85	92	98	115	131	148	164	181	197	230	263	296	319									
12	39/43	50	53	57	64	71	79	86	89	93	100	107	125	143	161	179	197	215	251	287	323										
15	49/53	62	67	71	80	89	98	107	111	116	125	134	157	179	202	224	247	268	314												
20	65/71	83	89	95	107	119	131	143	149	155	167	179	209	239	269	299	329														
25	82/89	104	111	119	134	149	164	179	187	194	209	224	262	299	337																
30	98/107	125	134	143	161	179	197	215	224	233	251	269	314																		

$3 Exacta Overlay Prices

	1/5	2/5	1/2	3/5	4/5	1	6/5	7/5	3/2	8/5	9/5	2	5/2	3	7/2	4	9/2	5	6	7	8	9	10	11	12	15	20	25	30	50	100
1/9																								6	6	8	10	12	14	23	46
1/5																		7	8	9	9	10	11	12	15	19	24	28	46	91
2/5														8	9	9	10	11	13	15	17	18	20	22	24	29	38	47	56	92	182
1/2												8	9	11	12	13	14	16	18	21	23	25	27	30	36	48	59	70	115	228
3/5										8	9	10	11	13	14	15	17	19	22	25	27	30	33	36	44	57	71	84	138	273
4/5							9	9	10	11	11	13	15	17	18	20	22	26	29	33	36	40	44	47	58	76	94	112	184	364
1						10	11	12	12	13	14	16	18	21	23	25	27	32	36	41	45	50	54	59	72	95	117	140	230	455
6/5					11	12	13	14	15	16	17	19	22	25	27	30	33	38	44	49	54	60	65	71	86	114	141	168	275	545
7/5				12	13	14	16	16	17	18	19	23	26	29	32	35	38	45	51	57	63	70	76	82	101	133	164	196	322	
3/2			13	14	15	17	17	18	19	21	24	27	31	34	38	41	48	54	61	68	75	81	88	108	142	176	210	345		
8/5			13	15	16	18	18	19	21	22	26	29	33	36	40	44	51	58	65	72	80	87	94	116	152	188	224	368		
9/5		13	15	17	18	20	21	22	23	25	29	33	37	41	45	49	57	65	73	81	90	98	106	130	171	211	252	413		
2		15	17	18	20	22	23	24	26	27	32	36	41	46	50	54	63	72	81	90	99	108	117	144	189	234	279	459		
5/2	17	18	21	23	25	27	29	30	32	34	40	45	51	57	62	68	79	90	102	113	124	135	147	180	237	293	349			
3	19	21	22	25	27	30	33	34	36	38	41	48	54	61	68	75	81	95	108	122	135	149	162	176	216	284	351	419			
7/2	23	24	26	29	32	35	38	40	41	45	48	56	63	71	79	87	95	111	126	142	158	174	189	205	252	331	419				
4	26	27	29	33	36	40	44	45	47	51	54	63	72	81	90	99	108	126	144	162	180	198	216	234	288	378	468				
9/2	29	31	33	37	41	45	49	51	53	57	61	71	81	92	102	112	122	142	162	183	203	223	243	264	324	426					
5	32	34	36	41	45	50	54	57	59	63	68	79	90	102	113	124	135	158	180	203	225	248	270	293	360	473					
6	33	38	41	44	49	54	60	65	68	71	76	81	95	108	122	135	149	162	189	216	243	270	297	324	351	432					
7	38	45	48	51	57	63	70	76	79	82	89	95	111	126	142	158	174	189	221	252	284	315	347	378	410	504					
8	44	51	54	58	65	72	80	87	90	94	101	108	126	144	162	180	198	216	252	288	324	360	396	432	468						
9	49	57	61	65	73	81	90	98	102	106	114	122	142	162	183	203	223	243	284	324	365	406	446	486	527						
10	50 / 55	54	68	72	81	90	99	108	113	117	126	136	158	180	203	226	248	270	315	360	405	450	495	540							
11	60 / 60	70	75	80	90	99	109	119	124	129	139	149	174	212	223	248	273	297	347	396	446	495	545								
12	65 / 75	76	81	87	98	108	119	130	135	141	152	162	189	216	243	270	297	324	378	432	486	540									
15	81 / 99	95	102	108	122	135	149	162	169	176	189	203	237	270	304	338	372	405	473	540											
20	108 / 124	126	135	144	162	180	198	216	225	234	252	270	315	360	405	450	495	540													
25	135 / 149	158	169	180	203	225	248	270	282	293	315	338	394	450	507	563															
30	162	189	203	216	243	270	297	324	338	351	378	405	473	540																	

$5 Exacta Overlay Prices

	1/5	2/5	1/2	3/5	4/5	1	6/5	7/5	3/2	8/5	9/5	2	5/2	3	7/2	4	9/2	5	6	7	8	9	10	11	12	15	20	25	30	50	100
1/9																							10	10	10	13	15	18	23	38	78
1/5																			10	10	12	13	15	17	18	23	30	38	45	78	153
2/5														10	12	13	15	18	20	23	25	28	33	38	40	50	65	80	95	155	305
1/2													12	13	15	18	20	20	23	28	30	35	40	43	45	58	78	95	115	193	380
3/5											12	13	15	18	20	20	23	25	30	35	40	43	48	55	60	70	93	115	138	228	453
4/5								12	13	15	15	18	20	23	25	28	33	35	40	45	53	58	65	70	78	95	125	158	188	308	605
1							15	17	18	19	20	20	25	28	33	35	40	43	50	58	65	73	80	88	95	118	155	193	230	380	
6/5						17	18	20	20	23	25	25	30	35	40	43	48	53	63	70	80	88	98	108	115	143	188	233	278	458	
7/5					20	20	23	25	25	28	28	30	35	40	45	50	58	63	73	83	93	103	115	125	135	168	220	273	325	535	
3/2				20	20	23	25	28	28	30	33	38	43	50	55	60	65	78	88	100	110	123	133	145	178	235	290	348	573		
8/5				20	23	25	28	28	30	33	35	40	45	53	58	65	70	83	95	108	118	130	143	155	190	250	310	370	610		
9/5			20	23	25	28	30	32	33	34	40	45	53	60	65	73	80	93	108	120	133	148	160	175	215	283	350	418	688		
2			23	25	28	30	33	35	36	40	43	50	58	65	73	80	88	103	118	133	148	163	178	193	238	313	388	463			
5/2		27	28	33	35	40	43	45	48	50	55	65	73	83	93	103	110	130	148	168	185	205	223	243	298	393	485	580			
3		30	33	40	43	48	53	55	58	63	65	78	88	100	110	123	133	155	178	200	223	245	268	290	358	470	583				
7/2	35	38	40	45	50	58	63	65	68	73	78	90	103	118	130	143	155	183	208	235	260	288	313	340	418	550	680				
4	40	43	45	53	58	65	70	73	78	83	88	103	118	133	148	163	178	208	238	268	298	328	358	388	478	628					
9/2	45	50	53	60	65	73	80	83	88	93	100	118	133	150	168	185	200	235	268	303	335	370	403	438	538						
5	50	55	58	65	73	80	88	93	95	103	110	122	148	168	185	205	223	260	298	335	373	410	448	485	598						
6	53	63	65	70	80	88	98	108	110	115	125	133	155	178	200	223	245	268	313	358	403	448	493	538	583						
7	63	73	78	83	93	103	115	125	130	135	145	155	183	208	235	260	288	313	365	418	470	523	575	628	680						
8	70	83	88	95	108	120	130	145	148	155	168	178	208	238	268	298	328	358	418	478	538	598	658								
9	80	93	100	108	120	133	148	160	168	175	188	200	235	268	303	335	370	403	470	538	605	673	740								
10	88	103	110	118	133	148	163	178	185	193	208	223	260	298	335	373	410	448	523	598	673	748									
11	98	115	123	130	148	163	180	198	205	213	230	245	288	328	370	410	453	493	575	658	740										
12	108	125	133	143	160	178	198	215	223	233	250	268	313	358	403	448	493	538	628	718											
15	123	133	155	168	178	200	223	245	268	278	290	313	335	393	448	505	560	618	673	785											
20	163	178	208	223	238	268	298	328	358	373	388	418	448	523	598	673	748														
25	205	223	260	278	298	335	373	410	448	468	485	523	560	655	748																
30	245	268	313	335	358	403	448	493	538	560	583	628	673	785																	

this chapter) onto which to copy the exacta possibilities that interest you. Attach a set of blanks to a clipboard.

On the left-hand side, above the large numbers, I list the odds I assign to each contender. This side reflects the race winner. On the top of the page go the same odds, this time representing the horse finishing second. Then, I put a long horizontal line through the number and across the page of any horse I've eliminated to win (though I may use this horse in the two-hole). In the remaining squares, I enter two payoffs:

1. In small numbers, at the top of each square, the number I require for that combination.
2. The price this combination is paying, which I enter about three minutes before post time.

I then circle every overlaid combination. These are the numbers I consider playing.

Let's say I make Silly Skipper 2-1 and Billy Bret 5-1. I need $35 to play Silly Skipper-Billy Bret and $44 for Billy Bret-Silly Skipper. If the numbers are below these, no play.

In some races I have no combinations circled. In others, I may have a dozen. Any time I have more than one combination playable close to post time, I subtract a losing minimum bet from each combination for every additional exacta I'm considering above one. If I have nine combinations circled in a race with a $2 betting minimum, for example, I subtract $16 (the cost of eight losing exacta bets) from every payoff. After doing this, I may have no combinations left, or only one, or maybe all nine. These are the ones I play.

If you don't subtract your losing exacta combinations, you may cash oodles of tickets while sustaining oodles of losses. While it's fun to collect a bet, it's dumb to throw away money just to brag you've located the cashiers window.

When you copy the numbers from the screen, ask:

1. *Is a horse being bet in exactas in proportion to its win odds?* Sometimes a horse has 20% of the win pool but only 15% of the exacta pool; an exacta wheel—usually an idiotic bet—would, with proportional betting, actually be preferable to a win wager.

2. *Are any numbers being suspiciously pounded?* Usually it doesn't take much to move a number so a drop from $70 to $32 shouldn't be worried over—but take this scenario: Bullet Bob, 10-1 in the morning line,

is being hammered to 9-5 and is also getting crushed in the exacta—but only with two horses, neither of which is the favorite. It's possible that funny business may be about.

    3. *Do values lurk among the many possible combinations?* This is our key question, for the answer to this will determine whether we play —and if so, for how much.

Your last decision will be how much to bet. This depends on several factors: the strength of your opinion about the race, the likelihood of the combination's winning (a $14 number will win far more often than a $96 number), the impact of your bet on the mutuel pool, the size of your bankroll, and the number of combos you are playing in a particular race.

Keep a separate exacta bankroll. With a $2,000 exacta fund, a 6% edge on a minimum overlay, and the .5 Kelly betting strategy (edge ÷ odds), the chart shows how much you can play if your track offers $2 exactas.

Exacta Bet Chart (Capital = $2000)	
Returning	**Bet**
$ 6 or less	$30
$ 7	$24
$ 8	$20
$ 9	$17
$10	$15
$11	$13
$12	$12
$13-14	$10
$15	$ 9
$16-17	$ 8
$18-19	$ 7
$20-22	$ 6
$23-26	$ 5
$27-32	$ 4
$33-42	$ 3
$43 +	$ 2

These numbers are minimums. Although the wagers may seem small, you may be betting several combinations in a race. In addition, large overlays demand a higher bet. For example, let's say you need $27 to bet

Exacta/Quinella Chart

	1	2	3	4	5	6	7	8	9	10	11	12
1	X											
2		X										
3			X									
4				X								
5					X							
6						X						
7							X					
8								X				
9									X			
10										X		
11											X	
12												X

	9/2 1	3 2	50 3	9/5 4	100 5	200 6	12 7	25 8	50 9	30 10	200 11	100 12
9/2 1	X	53 41	X	37 22	X	X	175 96	X	X	X	X	X
3 2	49 (51)	X	X	25 (33)	X	X	116 (132)	233 165	X	278 230	X	X
50 3												
9/5 4	29 18	21 (30)	275 133	X	X	X	70 58	140 97	X	167 126	X	X
100 5												
200 6												
12 7	197 138	143 112	X	100 75	X	X	X	X	X	X	X	X
25 8												
50 9												
30 10												
200 11												
100 12												

In this race, 3, 5, 6, 8, 9, 10, 11, and 12 are lineouts, so we don't even write down their combinations. Most other combos (e.g. 1-5, which is a 9-2 shot on top with a 100-1 shot second) are never overlaid and so are not listed on our $2 exacta overlay chart. We write all other needed overlay payoffs in small figures at the top of the appropriate box, then write the actual payoff from the TV monitor in large figures.

We circle the four overlaid combinations. However, after subtracting the three losing bets, the 2-1 becomes too low. We therefore play three combinations: 2-4, 2-7, and 4-2.

3-5 and it's on the board at $29; bet only $4. But if you need just $14 to bet 3-5 and it's returning $29, then bet $10 (the amount listed under "$13-14" in the chart) plus a bonus since your advantage is larger.

Other successful players use different methods. Some make one line for win bets and a completely separate one for second place, since certain bridesmaid types may fill out the exactas though they rarely win. Others wait for a race in which they like two horses only, then box them in either equal or varying amounts. Others use gauges or tables using the crowd's odds, rather than their own lines, on the theory that the crowd in general handicaps well but that overlays may lie in the exacta pools. Some harness bettors look for a lineup race (#5 leaves and the field lines up in post position order behind him, making 5-1, 5-2, and 5-3 the most likely winning combinations).

Whatever method you use, the lengthier the records you can compile, the better. Most exacta workouts I've seen are a joke. With 90 possible combinations coming up in every ten-horse field, paying amounts that may vary from $4 to $4,000, you'd need a workout of thousands of races before you could draw accurate conclusions.

A typical example: A researcher checks 500 exacta races and finds that playing the favorite in the two-hole with the next three choices yields a profit of 20%. Or does it? Perhaps the method clicked in 14% of the exacta races he checked, 70 winners paying a total of $1200 for the $1000 bet. What if two of those 70 winners paid over $100? What if only 11% of those exactas came in next time, a reasonable possibility?

There will be times when all kinds of bizarre plays seem to work for certain periods—boxing three horses, keying your third choice with every longshot, playing one front-runner with one closer—but before you believe any of it, give the method a workout. A very long workout.

The quinella, also called quiniela, is not nearly as popular as the exacta for a good reason—it's usually a worse bet. Let's say a player likes #4 to wire the field and figures that #1 and #2 are the most likely candidates for second. The exacta bettor can play 4-1 and 4-2. The quinella bettor also plays those numbers, but he collects less on a winning ticket and has to bet a possible finish of 1-4 and 2-4, neither of which he wants.

You can find quinella overlays from the chart on the next page. The 50% required bonus has been included. For example, to combine one horse you make 7-5 with another you list at 9-2 would require a probable

$2 Quinella Overlay Prices

	1	6/5	7/5	3/2	8/5	9/5	2	5/2	3	7/2	4	9/2	5	6	7	8	9	10	11	12	15	20	25	30	50	100
1/9																			4	4	4	5	7	10	14	29
1/5														4	4	4	4	5	5	6	7	10	12	15	25	50
2/5										4	4	4	4	5	6	7	8	9	10	11	14	18	23	28	46	92
1/2								4	4	4	4	5	5	7	8	9	10	11	12	13	17	22	28	34	56	111
3/5								4	4	4	5	6	6	8	9	10	12	13	14	16	20	26	33	39	65	130
4/5				4	4	4	4	5	6	7	8	8	10	12	13	15	17	18	20	25	33	42	50	83	165	
1			4	4	4	4	4	5	6	7	8	9	10	12	14	16	18	20	22	24	30	40	50	60	100	198
6/5		4	4	4	4	4	5	6	7	9	10	11	12	14	17	19	21	24	26	28	35	47	59	70	117	231
7/5			4	4	5	5	6	7	8	10	11	13	14	16	19	22	24	27	30	32	40	54	67	80	133	263
3/2				5	5	6	6	8	9	10	12	13	15	18	20	23	26	29	32	34	43	57	71	85	141	279
8/5				5	6	6	8	10	11	13	14	16	19	22	25	28	30	33	36	45	60	75	90	149	295	
9/5					7	7	9	11	12	14	16	17	21	24	27	31	34	37	40	50	67	83	99	165		
2						8	10	12	14	15	17	19	23	26	30	33	37	41	44	55	73	91	109	181		
5/2							12	14	17	19	21	23	28	32	36	41	45	50	54	67	89	111	133	220		
3								17	20	22	25	27	33	38	43	48	53	58	64	79	105	130	156	259		
7/2									23	26	29	32	38	43	49	55	61	67	73	91	120	150	179	298		
4										29	32	36	42	49	56	63	69	76	83	103	136	169	202			
9/2											36	40	47	55	62	70	77	85	92	114	151	188	225			
5												44	52	60	69	77	85	93	101	126	167	207	248			
6													62	72	81	91	101	111	120	149	198	246				
7														83	94	105	117	128	139	173	229	185				
8															107	120	133	145	158	196	260					
9																134	148	163	177	219	290					
10																	164	180	196	243						
11																		197	214	266						
12																			233	289						

payoff of $13 or higher assuming the quinella costs $2. As with the exacta, subtract all losing combos if you have more than one circled.

At a few tracks, both the quinella and exacta are offered in the same race, so shopping becomes a way of life. Using the 7-5 shot (X) with the 9-2 shot (Y), if the exactas were $19 for X-Y and $28 for Y-X (both too low) but the X-Y quinella was $14, bet the quinella only. At times you may play both the exacta and quinella; at other times, neither.

At some race books you can make a bet called the *house quinella.* This is computed by multiplying the win price of the first-place finisher by half the place price of the second-place finisher. This bet is most attractive in short fields where you have two solid favorites who figure to bury the rest of the field.

Even though I recommend making a line for every horse and using it to ferret out overlays, you can still use both the exacta and quinella charts even if you do not make a line and choose to accept the crowd's line as accurate. As a rough approximation, simply move all requirements over by two columns in each direction. For example, the crowd makes your two top picks (call them Secretariat and Citation) 6-5 and 5-2. *Do not* use the 6-5 to 5-2 square for the Secretariat-Citation exacta. Instead, use the 3-2 to 7-2 square. Thus you'd need $20 for this $2 exacta, and $10 for this $2 quinella.

An occasional track offers a bet in which you must select two consecutive exactas or quinellas. Without knowing the possible payoffs, it's difficult to determine whether this is a play of value.

To summarize our exacta/quinella plan:
1. *Analyze the race,* making an odds line.
2. *Find the combinations that interest you,* marking their required overlay prices from the tables.
3. *Check the payoffs* on the monitor.
4. *Circle all overlays.* If more than one, deduct the cost per ticket of all additional bets (e.g., if 12 combinations are circled at a track with a $3 minimum exacta bet, deduct 11 x $3 from each payoff).
5. *Play all remaining combinations* using the appropriate bet chart.

TRIFECTAS

While picking the 1-2-3 order of finish in a race isn't easy, the hard part is that you must bet without knowing whether you're getting value.

Unlike exactas and quinellas, when you play trifectas (also called triactors), you usually have no idea what the numbers you fancy will pay. You don't know whether you're betting an overlay or an underlay. Is the 2-4-7 combination returning $68 or $680? All you know is you're bucking a 25% takeout on a blind bet.

That makes the trifecta a much less desirable play than the exacta and quinella. Add integrity questions to the mix (Is Smith dead on the favorite? Will Jones wake up the longshot for a score?) and you've got real problems with the trifecta.

Nonetheless, trifectas do offer the one edge that is characteristic of all exotic wagers—the throwaway factor. Thank you, numerology and astrology players. Others spread wildly, buying so many tickets that they lose money even when they hit the winning combination. These donations mean free money for sharp players.

Before deciding whether to play the trifecta, decide whether the race interests you. At tracks where only one or two trifectas a day are offered, there's a temptation to play the tri even when the event is a maiden race featuring six first-time starters or a $2500 claimer where the entire field can't go forward. If you don't like the race well enough to make a line on it, forget the trifecta. This helps avoid such desperado strategies as boxing a bunch and hoping something long comes in.

Trifecta costs can escalate rapidly. Wheel one horse in a nine-horse race and a $2 trifecta costs $112, which is more than it might pay. While it's true that occasionally a trifecta comes back in five figures, usually the number is considerably less. If your entire betting stake is only $500, don't bother with the trifecta at all—it will require too high a percentage of your bankroll to play properly.

Looking over a large number of trifecta results, one notes the influence of the $1 box bet on the size of the payoffs. When the favorites finish 1-2-3 in any order, the return is miniscule—you're better off taking a shot at the exacta. Occasionally a trifecta will even return less than an exacta.

The biggest returns take place when some bizzarro sneaks into the trifecta. But the two most common strategies—boxing and wheeling—are dismal failures. Boxing (taking your top three, four, or five horses and betting them in all orders) generally yields underlaid payoffs even if the favorite finishes third.

A better strategy for the trifecta, as it is with the exacta, is to key your top horse for first (and sometimes second) with the legitimate contenders —not merely throw the horse in with everybody and pray. To catch big payoffs, use a strange one in the third slot, since even living filth may stagger in third with the right trip.

For example, let's say you like #2 best, #4 next best, and give #1, #5, and #8 small shots. Your play may look like this:

```
                    2—4—1
                    2—4—5
                    2—4—8
                    2—4—1356789
                    2—1—4
                    2—5—4
                    2—8—4
                    2—1356789—4
                    2—1—356789
                    2—5—136789
                    2—8—135679
                    4—2—1
                    4—2—5
                    4—2—8
                    4—2—1356789
                    1—2—3456789
                    5—2—1346789
                    8—2—1345679
```

Assuming a nine-horse race, $2 tickets on each combination would cost $138. If you figured the race correctly (#2 winning with #4 second or third), you'd have either one or two winning tickets. You'd also have one or two winners if #4 defeated #2. If one of your outsiders managed to beat #2, you'd still collect. Ditto if #2 won and one of your outsiders was second, even if #4 ran out.

With this type of ticket, you'd always collect something if your horse finished first or second with one of your contenders first or second. You'd also have a chance at a giant payoff. You'd miss if your horse finished third, or something weird snuck in the place hole unless your second choice also finished third.

The major problem with this play, however, is that you're betting a lot of combinations. With a strong opinion—you love #5, think that at least one of #1, #2, or #3 must finish in the money and feel #8 and #9 are so horrible they couldn't get into the picture even with fudging in the photo lab—you can play fewer combinations in larger amounts:

5—1—2
5—1—3
5—2—1
5—2—3
5—3—1
5—3—2
5—1—23467
5—2—13467
5—3—12467
5—23467—1
5—13467—2
5—12467—3

For only $72, you'll win at least once if you're right, and twice if two of your horses finish in the money. If you feel especially strongly about certain things (e.g., #1 or #2 look like virtual cinches to finish in the money), you can play extra combinations on certain tickets.

This comes down to the basic philosophy of the trifecta—are you playing merely to hit it, or to make a score? If you're looking to crush, bet more money on fewer combinations. If you typically bet three exacta combinations, you shouldn't bet more than 15 trifecta combos.

One of the best things about the trifecta is that unlike the daily double or other multiple-win exotics, you need be right only once. Let's say, for example, that as you analyze a harness race you see #3 and #5 lining up 1-2 around the track, slowing the pace. You can then eliminate anybody from the outside posts and bet big using 3-5 and 5-3, and 3-others-5 and 5-others-3. If you're right, you'll bury the number.

Without a key horse or horses, don't play the trifecta. You've got to focus —one horse must run either first or second and something else must happen (even if it's only one of a certain group of five horses must finish second).

Once you've decided on your combinations, write them down—don't expect to merely call them off a program or you'll invariably forget to include the one number that hits. Learn the terminology (e.g., "Part-wheel 1 with 3-4-6 for second and 2-5-9 for third," etc.) to make your transactions smooth.

Get on line early before trifecta races, since betting the tri takes more time than making simple win or exacta bets. If just one or two people ahead of you take an inordinate amount of time, you could get shut out.

Many tracks let you bet $1 trifectas, at least in boxes or partial wheels. This can become important when the payoff for $2 is, say, $1100. Had you bet the combination for $2, you would have lost 20% for withholding and had to fill out an I.R.S. slip. But by betting only $1 twice, you can cash both tickets at $550 apiece and avoid the hassle. If you're planning to bet the same combination for, say, $8, and it's a number that could easily pay over $600 for $2, bet the combination for $1 and ask the clerk to press the "repeat" button on his machine eight times. (If the combination consists of three favorites and figures to pay $80 for $2, of course, this would merely be a waste of time.)

If you like a longshot in the trifecta, you're usually better off betting him to win instead. However, if you're planning to bet a large enough amount on the longshot that its odds would no longer make it an overlay, you might bet some in the win pool and some in the trifecta.

At dog tracks, the threat of trifecta fixes is minimal—and the bet has flourished at many of them. Since dog tracks also offer frequent quinellas, *Racing Greyhounds* editor Gordon Waite has developed a $2 trifecta estimation payoff chart, which appears below. Simply take the quinella odds on your first- and second-place dogs (e.g., if a combination is paying $26 then the quinella odds are 12-1), look up the win odds of the third dog, then find the square for the payoff estimation. If you are making a $1 bet, of course, divide this number in half.

Let's say you're betting the 3-8-2 trifecta combination. If the 3-8 quinella is paying $12 and the 2 dog is 8-1 on the board, then the trifecta estimate for the 3-8-2 combination is $130. If you're betting 5-4-6 and the 5-4 quinella is paying $32 and the 6 dog is 9-1, the estimated trifecta payoff is $609.

$2 Trifecta Estimator

		2	3	4	5	6	7	8	9	10	12	15	20	25	26 +
	11 +	132	181	224	253	268	282	449	582	621	676	708	1153	1202	2165
	10	96	145	179	230	227	252	316	483	501	611	657	1006	1150	2125
	9	90	138	158	135	207	230	255	284	372	514	609	954	1065	1899
	8	86	117	127	130	160	190	242	272	347	424	568	836	967	1773
Win	7	82	101	121	128	141	180	186	247	335	362	504	702	806	1623
Odds	6	76	85	110	112	135	164	178	225	304	310	483	616	767	1504
on	5	65	82	100	101	119	155	168	201	241	301	416	429	655	1296
Third	4	59	78	67	86	112	118	148	186	193	279	369	398	578	1198
Dog	3	43	54	46	69	102	112	136	154	168	222	325	373	545	1073
	2	x	42	43	53	82	96	107	129	148	154	207	360	501	872
	1	x	x	39	41	63	83	95	118	123	138	177	287	443	701

Quinella Odds On First & Second Dogs

At a few tracks you can play the superfecta, picking the first four finishers in order. It is easy to overbet, however, as costs mount rapidly in this bet unless you require certain results, as in #3 must win and #4 must finish in the top 4. (Even so, in a nine-horse race this ticket would cost $294 using $2 bets.) It is easy to either throw away dozens of small tickets, or bet too high a percentage of your bankroll using large ones, in a vain attempt to try to hit the superfecta. If you do succeed, the I.R.S. will once again be waiting for you.

Some tracks offer a twin trifecta. In this event, you must hit two consecutive trifectas, and payoffs sometimes run into six figures. This and similar wagers such as the super bet (two exactas followed by a trifecta) are strictly plays for big bettors on carryover days. Small players trying to hit the twin tri invariably wind up missing, contributing to the cash flow of the heavy hitters who can afford four-figure investments.

THE DAILY DOUBLE

While the daily double qualifies as a multiple win exotic in that you must pick winners in consecutive races, it enjoys a large edge over pick 3's, pick 4's, and pick 6's. Unlike those plays, daily double odds are clearly posted before you bet—so you can determine whether a combination is an overlay.

The mathematics of daily double play are simple. Multiply the win chances of your contenders in the first half by the win chances of those you like in the second half to determine fair odds, then add the overlay requirement. All the work is done for you by the chart on page 83.

For example, let's say you make Lucky Larry 3-1 (25% win chance) in the first and Battling Bertha 4-1 in the second (20% win chance). Multiplying .25 x .20 gives us .05, which is the chance that both horses will win. Fair odds for this combination, then, are 19-1. Our 50% bonus requirement raises this to 28.5 to 1, or $59. If the $2 payoff on the monitor says $59 or higher, the double of Lucky Larry to Battling Bertha is playable.

Just as with exacta bets, subtract your losing plays before making your final plays. For example, if the Lucky Larry-Battling Bertha double was listed at $61 but you had seven additional playable combinations, subtract $14 (the seven losing bets) from each payoff. That would bring this double to $47, too low to play.

$2 Daily Double Overlay Prices

	1/9	1/5	2/5	1/2	3/5	4/5	1	6/5	7/5	3/2	8/5	9/5	2	5/2	3	7/2	4	9/2	5	6	7	8	9	10	11	12	15	20	25
1/9	4	4	4	4	4	5	6	6	7	7	8	8	9	11	12	14	16	17	19	22	26	29	32	36	39	42	52	69	86
1/5		4	4	4	5	5	6	7	8	8	8	9	10	12	13	15	17	19	21	24	28	31	35	39	42	46	57	75	93
2/5			5	5	6	7	7	8	9	10	10	11	12	14	16	18	20	22	24	28	33	37	41	45	50	54	66	87	108
1/2				6	6	7	8	9	10	10	11	12	13	15	17	19	22	24	26	31	35	40	44	49	53	58	71	94	116
3/5					7	8	9	10	11	11	11	12	13	16	18	21	23	25	28	33	37	42	47	52	57	61	76	100	124
4/5						9	10	11	12	12	13	14	15	18	21	23	26	29	31	37	42	48	53	58	64	69	85	112	139
1							11	12	13	14	15	16	17	20	23	26	29	32	35	41	47	53	59	65	71	77	95	125	154
6/5								14	15	16	16	17	19	22	25	29	32	35	39	45	52	58	65	72	78	85	105	138	170
7/5									16	17	18	19	21	24	28	31	35	39	42	49	57	64	71	78	85	93	114	150	186
3/2										18	19	20	22	25	29	33	37	40	44	51	59	67	74	82	89	96	119	157	194
8/5											19	21	22	26	30	34	38	42	46	54	62	69	77	85	93	100	124	163	202
9/5												23	24	28	33	37	41	45	49	58	66	75	83	91	100	108	133	176	217
2													26	31	35	40	44	48	53	62	71	80	89	98	107	116	143	188	233
5/2														36	41	46	52	57	62	72	83	94	104	115	125	136	167	220	272
3															47	53	59	65	71	83	95	107	119	131	143	155	191	251	311
7/2																60	67	73	80	93	107	121	134	148	161	175	215	283	350
4																	74	81	89	104	119	134	149	164	179	194	239	314	389
9/2																		90	98	114	131	147	164	180	197	213	263	345	427
5																			107	125	143	161	179	197	215	233	286	377	466
6																				146	167	188	209	230	251	272	335	440	544
7																					191	215	239	263	287	311	383	503	622
8																						242	269	296	323	350	431	566	700
9																							299	329	359	389	479	629	778
10																								362	395	428	527	692	856
11																									431	467	575	756	934
12																										506	623	819	1012
15																											767	1007	1246
20																												1323	1636
25																													2022

The blank sheet we attach to our clipboard is similar to the one we use for the exacta and quinella, but without the diagonal line in the middle (you can't have a 3-3 exacta; you certainly can have a 3-3 daily double). On the left-hand side go your own round-book odds of the first-race contenders. Write the second-race contenders' odds on top. Check the table for the payoffs required. Then copy the numbers from the monitors, circle the overlays, and head to the windows—remembering, of course, to bet at the last possible second to see those late odds.

In the example daily double in this chapter, our 100% round-book odds lines are:

1st Race		2nd Race	
# 1...	25-1 (lineout)	# 1...	4-5
# 2...	5-2	# 2...	25-1 (lineout)
# 3...	3-1	# 3...	50-1 (lineout)
# 4...	11-1	# 4...	100-1 (lineout)
# 5...	100-1 (lineout)	# 5...	6-1
# 6...	100-1 (lineout)	# 6...	200-1 (lineout)
# 7...	9-1	# 7...	30-1 (lineout)
# 8...	200-1 (lineout)	# 8...	12-1
# 9...	7-1	# 9...	200-1 (lineout)
#10...	20-1 (lineout)	#10...	200-1 (lineout)
#11...	200-1 (lineout)	#11...	200-1 (lineout)
#12...	30-1 (lineout)	#12...	9-1

With horizontal lines, we discard those horses that we've eliminated from the first race. With vertical lines, we bounce the second-race lineouts. We've left in five contenders in the first race and four in the second, so we need to write in requirements for 20 combinations.

We enter the demands in small print in the top section of the appropriate square. Then, as the numbers appear on the monitors in the last minutes before post time, we fill in our 20 boxes.

In this race, we have four combinations remaining: 3-1, 3-5, 7-1, and 7-5. Subtracting $6 from each combination because of the excess number of combos (3 extras multiplied by $2 per combo), we are left with only 3-1 and 7-1.

Note that while our top choice in the second race is on both tickets, in the first half of the double we're playing only our second choice and our fourth choice. That will happen frequently. We always seek overlays, not just winners. Any combination of contenders is playable.

The 3-12 combo is just a dollar short of being circled. When you begin to record the numbers, about five minutes to post time, pay special attention to numbers which are either just above, or just below, the cutoff point. It's possible that on the last flash, 3-1 might be banged down to just $22 (which would then render it unplayable after subtraction) and 3-12 might drift up to $137 (which would make it playable). Observe the TV screen as you wait on line to bet, aware that your final play won't be determined until the last moment.

As for how much to bet on the double, we'll use the same table we used for exactas, again assuming a separate $2000 daily double bankroll with a 6% edge on a minimum overlay, a .5 Kelly betting strategy, and $2 doubles.

Daily Double Bet Chart
(Capital = $2000)

Returning	Bet
$ 6 or less	$30
$ 7	$24
$ 8	$20
$ 9	$17
$10	$15
$11	$13
$12	$12
$13-14	$10
$15	$ 9
$16-17	$ 8
$18-19	$ 7
$20-22	$ 6
$23-26	$ 5
$27-32	$ 4
$33-42	$ 3
$43+	$ 2

These numbers are minimums. Large overlays demand a higher bet, and you'll often play several combinations.

Sometimes, you'll have to pass the double even though you love both races. Let's say you have a solid horse in the first you make 1-1, and three contenders in the second that you assess at 5-2, 5-2, and 3-1. If the crowd

Daily Double Chart

	1	2	3	4	5	6	7	8	9	10	11	12
1												
2												
3												
4												
5												
6												
7												
8												
9												
10												
11												
12												

Daily Double Chart

	4/5 1	25 2	50 3	190 4	6 5	240 6	30 7	12 8	200 9	200 10	200 11	9 12
25 1												
5/2 2	19 15				72 49			136 88				104 100
3 3	21 (28)				83 (85)			155 124				119 118
11 4	64 55				251 204			467 373				359 301
100 5												
100 6												
9 7	53 (71)				209 (209)			389 326				299 270
200 8												
7 9	42 36				167 140			311 252				239 175
20 10												
200 11												
30 12												

puts up numbers like $15, $16, and $19, you're out of business—even if you rated both races as A's. As with other bets, the plan is to make money, not simply to cash tickets.

Occasionally you may key one horse in the double while betting a different horse to win. Each bet is separate—if one horse is an overlay to win while another horse in the race is an overlay in the double pool, then you may wind up playing both. This may prove confusing to your rooting but is nevertheless the best way to maximize profits.

Through *proportional betting*, the double pool sometimes will yield an overlay that the win pool may not. Let's say that you need 2-1 to bet Mighty Mosquito in the first race, but he's only 8-5 on the board. You've narrowed the second race to five contenders, but the race doesn't interest you much and you haven't made a line for it. That keeps you from the search for dd overlays. However, the payoffs with Mighty Mosquito are $20, $42, $44, $65, and $98:

$20 (9-1)	10% of round book
$42 (20-1)	5% of round book
$44 (21-1)	5% of round book
$65 (31-1)	3% of round book
$98 (48-1)	2% of round book
Total:	25% of round book (odds of 3-1)

If you bet $100 proportionally in the double, assuming your horse wins the first and allowing that a non-contender will upset in the second half 20% of the time, you'll get the following return:

20% of the time = return of zero
80% of the time = return of $400 (approximately)

For each five sequences, your total bet will be $500 and your expected return will be $1600. Thus you can lock in odds of 2.2 to 1 on Mighty Mosquito in the first. (You can also use this technique if your horse is in the second race.)

If either race in the pair seems questionable, do not search for overlays (although you may lock in minimum odds, as above). At many tracks, the daily double consists of the two worst races on the card. While this is not always a problem (a $5000 claimer may be eminently playable), from time to time you'll come across a race that you simply hate. Even if you love the other half of the double, pass.

If your track offers the daily double in its first two races, don't arrive with five minutes to post. Not only won't you have time to analyze the races, but you won't be able to watch horses in the paddock and you might miss a crucial late jockey change. It's tough enough making money without adding in sloppy work.

Never play a double just to have some action going. Everything you do is guided by one question—*will it help you make money*? If the numbers are good, play. If not, pass.

Think of the dd pool as one more potential source of cash. Let's say you play at a small track that handles only $300,000 a day. The first race offers the usual win, place, and show wagering. The win pool may total only $8,000. It's hard to play for more than 10% of a pool (your bets will influence the odds severely if you do), so it would be difficult to grab more than $800 on the win end.

But perhaps the track handles another $8,000 in the exacta and an additional $8,000 in the daily double. Now you're looking at a potential win of $2,400 (10% of the $24,000 total). You can make a lot of money by being right in a race that offers exotic betting.

MULTIPLE WIN EXOTICS—THE PICK 3

The bets described in this chapter and the next have two features in common—you must pick a certain number of winners in consecutive races, and you have no access to possible payoffs. They've been around in various incarnations for more than 20 years, though some wrinkles are relatively recent. Collectively, these bets are known as *multiple win exotics* (mwe's).

They have various names, but to avoid confusion, we'll call them pick 3's, pick 4's, and pick 6's. (Example: The pick 3 is called the triple at some tracks, but at others the term "triple" means trifecta.)

Not discussed in these pages are plays such as twin quinellas, twin exactas, twin trifectas, and the super bet. Few tracks offer them. And most are better left to investment groups that can afford to wait for carryovers and then play huge tickets. (One clique would fly to whatever track offered a giant carryover and bet thousands of dollars—sometimes tens of thousands—in an effort to hit. The team was barred from Sportsman's Park because track officials felt the team's being able to bet so much capital gave it an unfair advantage over local bettors. But of course —that was the whole idea!)

Whether to play a particular pick 3, pick 4, or pick 6 (not recommended are bets requiring you to pick more than six winners) depends on several factors:
- Amount of the pool, including carryover
- Odds of hitting that day's mwe

- Size of the bet necessary to attain those odds
- Your opinion on the races involved

In this chapter, we'll examine the pick 3. In the next, we'll look at pick 4's and pick 6's.

The pick 3 came to California in 1986 and became an immediate success. Daily doubles are easier to select but don't pay as much, while pick 6's are difficult to catch and require a large investment. The pick 3 seems to offer something for everybody—a fair likelihood of hitting, combined with the chance of an occasional five-figure payoff.

Though the takeout may be 25% for the pick 3, it's a takeout that stretches over three races. That makes the pick 3 far superior to a parlay. Let's study exactly what effect that takeout has by looking at three $2 pick 3 plays where on your line the winners are (1) 1-1, 1-1, and 1-1 (2) 3-1, 3-1, and 3-1 (3) 9-1, 9-1, and 9-1:

Three 1-1 Shots	**Three 3-1 Shots**	**Three 9-1 Shots**
No take $16.00	No take $128.00	No take . . . $2000.00
25% take $12.00	25% take . . . $ 96.00	25% take . . $1500.00
16% parlay. . . $ 8.20	16% parlay. . $ 71.80	16% parlay $1184.40

The pick 3 requires a different strategy from both the daily double (where you can find overlays) and the pick 6 (where hitting all 6 one time is the goal). And since the pick 3 is relatively new, few players have thought about what that strategy might be.

Let's look at some of the incorrect approaches. Wheeling in the pick 3 is just like wheeling in the exacta or the double—you don't like every horse in the race equally, so why bet them all equally? Wheeling comes from a losing mindset that thinks, "I love this horse in the first leg, so I'll use him with everything so if he wins I won't blow the pick 3."

Sure, sometimes you'll key one horse, he'll win, and you'll miss the pick 3 because you left out some longie—but so what? Many studies have shown that you'll lose far more money betting every 50-1 shot than betting every 3-5 shot, and you'll certainly be throwing away money in the long term by wheeling. Instead, play your key horses with your contenders—not with everything that moves. If you absolutely hate the thought of losing a bet when your key horse wins, then just bet the horse to win and forget the exotics.

Neither can you expect to combine every conceivable live horse in all three races on one large ticket and net a long-term profit. Assuming you narrow each race to four horses, and 80% of the time one of those four horses wins, this incorrect play will require 64 combinations (at $2 or $3 per combo, depending on the track) and will hit 51%—far below the percentage you'd need to rake in net profits using that many combinations with what are mostly low-odds horses.

Usually, the public bets each horse in the pick 3 in about the same ratio as it does in the win pool—so, assuming you handicap as well as the public (and most players don't, since betting all public favorites yields less of a loss than betting one horse per race indiscriminately), you won't make money on the pick 3.

But several situations yield potential pick 3 profits—and if you restrict your action to these circumstances, you can do well:
1. The public is certain to overbet a horse you hate.
2. The public is certain to underbet a horse you like.
3. At least one and preferably two of the races are wide open, which will eliminate small bettors who can afford to use only the top one or two choices.

In all these cases, you are looking to gain an edge over the public. *Without an edge, there is no point in playing the pick 3.* If you like the same horses as everyone else, to the same degree, skip the pick 3. Just as you'd pass a 4-5 shot if you think his odds are too low, even if he's the most likely winner, don't play unless you feel you'll get value.

For example, take this potential pick 3 play:

1st race —Three evenly matched horses battle eight others, none of whom look especially promising.
2nd race—Two solid standouts and three other horses with a chance face five others who appear hopeless.
3rd race—An obvious 2-5 shot should romp.

Do not play this pick 3, since everybody in the stands will have a similar ticket, and there's no ticket that will give you an edge.

So what? you might ask. Who cares if everybody else cashes as long as I do, too? Wrong, wrong, wrong.

Let's look at the percentages. In the first heat, we figure that the three favorites will win 80% of the time. In the second, the standouts might win 60% with the next three choices taking 25% for a total of 85%. In the third, the 2-5 shot will win about 65% of the time. So even if we play all the obvious horses ($3 \times 5 \times 1$), we're going to win this bet only 44% of the time. If the pick 3 costs $2, we'll be betting $30 and we'll need a payoff of about $68 merely to break even and $102 for a 50% bonus—more than this ticket would return.

If we play only the top two in the second heat, we'll cash only 31% of the time. Our cost is now only $12, but the payoff needs to average $39 for us to make a profit and $58 with the bonus requirement—unlikely with all obvious horses.

But if you handicap the races differently from what the crowd probably will do, then you can gain an advantage. Let's say, for instance, that you're not especially thrilled with the 2-5 shot. You know the crowd will make him 2-5 but you don't think he's worth lower than 6-5. Maybe he's a horse that loves to finish second, or his fast speed rating was accomplished because of a misleading pace, or the trainer is 1-for-40 with horses in similar circumstances. Now you can play—by throwing the horse out.

Throw out a 2-5 shot? Even though you still make him 6-5 to win the race? Absolutely—since this is your chance to beat the crowd. If the horse wins, the pick 3 will be worth nothing anyway. But if he's beaten, you'll get excellent value since every small player (and some big ones) may be singling him. Better to use your next choice (or two, or three) on this ticket and hope the favorite loses.

You can also gain an edge when you think the public will neglect a horse you like. For instance, you feel a horse should be 3-1, but his past-performance lines look deceptively poor and you're sure he'll be at least 5-1. Not only can you gain an edge in the win pool, but the pick 3 could prove a bonanza. The public will almost certainly underbet him in the pick 3, so you may get good value if he wins (I say "may" instead of "will," because the horse could win and you still can miss the pick 3; those are the breaks).

Let's look at the three example races in a different handicapping light:

1st race—Three evenly matched horses battle eight others, none of whom look especially promising.

But it's the first event of the pick 3 and the crowd is making one of the three horses 6-5. *Strategy*: Since they're probably also overbetting him in the pick 3, throw him out and use the other two only.

> 2nd race—Two solid standouts and three other horses with a chance face five others who appear hopeless.

You can't separate the top two, but you think the crowd will overbet one of the other three. *Strategy*: When making out your tickets, throw out the one you think will be overbet.

> 3rd race—An obvious 2-5 shot should romp.

If you agree that he should romp, single him. If you make him 6-5 and are not crazy about him, throw him out and use your next one, two, or three choices instead.

Rarely do I put in one large ticket on a pick 3. Instead, I calculate what the chances are of each combination's clicking, then make the tickets out accordingly. For example, here would be a typical scenario, with the horse number listed first and what chance I think he has of winning in parentheses:

    1st —#4 (40%), #3 (25%), #1 (20%)...............3 (85%)
    2nd—#7 (45%), #6 (15%), #9 (10%), #5 (10%).....4 (80%)
    3rd —#2 (25%), #8 (25%), #3 (12%), others small...3 (62%)

If I think the public will figure each of the races the same way, I put in no ticket at all (even though a $3 \times 4 \times 3$ ticket would win 42% of the time). I have no edge.

The same is true even if I just use top choices (doubling in the last). A ticket of 4-7-28 would cost $4 (assuming $2 pick 3's) but would win only 9% of the time. A $45 payoff would barely break even and the overlay price would be $67—a highly unlikely average return here.

When you play the pick 3, take into account how much you like each horse in each race. For example, in the first race above we give #4 a 40% chance to win while we think #1 has only a 20% chance. Therefore, we should have a higher percentage of our total investment using #4 rather than #1.

Before putting in a pick 3 ticket, I ask the following:
  1. Are my choices the same as the public's?
  2. If not, what are my S/A/B possibilities?

S/A/B assumes that every horse in a pick 3 falls into one of four categories:

S . . . . *Single*—horse you like best with no backup.

A . . . . *Above the line*—your top choice or choices, though not worth being singled.

B . . . . *Below the line*—contenders you like as chance plays, not as good as your A horses.

Others. . . . Horses you've *eliminated*.

By placing each horse into one of these categories, you can construct tickets that will reflect how you feel about that day's pick 3.

Pick 3's are playable only if the local rule permits a substitution (either your own choice or the post-time favorite) in case of a scratch; in some places, if you hit the first two winners in a pick 3 and your horse is scratched from the third, all you get back is your bet using that horse —outrageous if you've gone $8 \times 8 \times 1$ and gotten home two 50-1 shots, only to lose $62 on your play ($64 minus your $2 refund).

Let's make out some tickets. Take the following pick 3:

> 1st —#2 (55%)
> 2nd—#1 (40%) #2 (20%), #6 (16%), #7 (12%)
> 3rd—#4 (50%), #3 (30%)

One big ticket costing $16 would have a 38.7% chance of hitting. For a 50% overlay, this ticket must pay $62 or higher; but it won't unless two longer-priced horses win.

Instead of playing one big ticket, you might insist that one of your top choices win either the second or the third in addition to your first-race single. That would give you the following combinations:

> 2-1-4 (11.0% chance)
> 2-1-3 (6.6% chance)
> 2-2-4 (5.5% chance)
> 2-6-4 (4.4% chance)
> 2-7-4 (3.3% chance)

Using five combinations only would give you a 30.8% chance to hit, and a payoff of just $49 would be an overlay. And by separating the combinations and figuring their win chances, you can choose to bet higher on those with a greater chance of hitting. For example, if you wanted to invest approximately $90 in this pick 3, multiply by 3 for the following $91 investment:

$$
\begin{array}{ll}
\text{2-1-4} \ldots\ldots\ldots\ldots & \$33 \\
\text{2-1-3} \ldots\ldots\ldots\ldots & \$19 \\
\text{2-2-4} \ldots\ldots\ldots\ldots & \$16 \\
\text{2-6-4} \ldots\ldots\ldots\ldots & \$13 \\
\text{2-7-4} \ldots\ldots\ldots\ldots & \$10 \\
\end{array}
$$

Each set of charts below consists of two portions:

1. How to make out pick 3 tickets based on how many singles (S) and other top choices (A) must win.
2. The number of combinations necessary. This number must be multiplied by $1, $2, or $3 depending on the cost per ticket at your track.

All figures regarding number of combinations assume that the above-the-line horse (A) is your top pick only. Your costs mount as A is increased to two or three horses.

The names of each ticket sequence (0A, 1A, or 2A) refer to the number of A's (top choices) which must win the non-singled races. For each bet, 0A is the number of combinations necessary to put in one giant ticket using all contenders (even though for each 0A, the key says "one more" which consists of all B's winning). The ticket cost of 3A's is always one combination, so it is not listed (although how to make that ticket out is).

If you do not separate your B's, the maximum number of tickets you would play is eight. Take the following pick 3:

      1st —#2 (40%), #7 (20%), #3 (12%)
      2nd—#8 (45%), #1 (20%), #6 (14%), #7 (10%)
      3rd —#4 (50%), #3 (15%), #9 (15%)

The no-singles chart for 3-3-4 (the number of horses you've left in for each race) shows eight tickets with 36 total combinations. The tickets would be made out as follows:

$$
\begin{array}{lll}
\text{AAA} \ldots & \text{2-8-4} \ldots\ldots\ldots\ldots & \text{1 combination} \\
\text{AAB} \ldots & \text{2-8-39} \ldots\ldots\ldots & \text{2 combinations} \\
\text{ABA} \ldots & \text{2-167-4} \ldots\ldots\ldots & \text{3 combinations} \\
\text{BAA} \ldots & \text{73-2-4} \ldots\ldots\ldots & \text{2 combinations} \\
\text{ABB} \ldots & \text{2-167-39} \ldots\ldots\ldots & \text{6 combinations} \\
\text{BAB} \ldots & \text{73-8-39} \ldots\ldots\ldots & \text{4 combinations} \\
\text{BBA} \ldots & \text{73-167-4} \ldots\ldots\ldots & \text{6 combinations} \\
\text{BBB} \ldots & \text{73-167-39} \ldots\ldots & \text{12 combinations} \\
\end{array}
$$

Number of Pick 3 Combinations Necessary

S....single
A....above-the-line or top choice
B....below-the-line or secondary choice

1 single

2A (1 ticket)
1st... A
2nd...A
3rd... S

1A (2 more = 3)
1st... A B
2nd...B A
3rd... S S

0A (1 more = 4)
1st... B
2nd...B
3rd... S

	1A	0A
S22	3	4
S23	4	6
S24	5	8
S25	6	10
S26	7	12
S33	5	9
S34	6	12
S35	7	15
S36	8	18
S44	7	16
S45	8	20
S46	9	24
S55	9	25
S56	10	30
S66	11	36

0 singles

3A (1 ticket)
1st... A
2nd...A
3rd... A

2A (3 more = 4)
1st... A A B
2nd...A B A
3rd... B A A

1A (3 more = 7)
1st... A B B
2nd...B A B
3rd... B B A

0A (1 more = 8)
1st... B
2nd...B
3rd... B

	2A	1A	0A		2A	1A	0A
222	4	7	8	336	10	34	54
223	5	10	12	344	9	30	48
224	6	13	16	345	10	36	60
225	7	16	20	346	11	42	72
226	8	20	24	355	11	43	75
233	6	14	18	356	12	50	90
234	7	18	24	366	13	58	108
235	8	22	30	444	10	37	64
236	9	26	36	445	11	44	80
244	8	23	32	446	12	51	96
245	9	28	40	455	12	52	100
246	10	33	48	456	13	60	120
255	10	34	50	466	14	69	140
256	11	40	60	555	13	61	125
266	12	47	72	556	14	70	150
333	7	19	27	566	15	80	180
334	8	24	36	666	16	91	216
335	9	29	45				

By insisting that at least one of your A's win, you would slash the required number of combinations from 36 to 24 (eliminating the final ticket). See the chart that says "1A, 334" and you'll find the number there is 24.

I always separate my B's, however, to try to come up with tickets that exactly reflect how I feel about each race. Since in the first race, for example, I like #3 much less than #7, I'll weight my tickets more heavily with #7.

Take, for instance, the BAB ticket of 73-8-39. Overall, that ticket has a 4.3% chance to win ($32\% \times 45\% \times 30\%$). However, 7-8-39 has a 2.7% chance ($20\% \times 45\% \times 30\%$) while 3-8-39 has only a 1.6% chance ($12\% \times 45\% \times 30\%$). So I'll bet more on the 7-8-39 combination, trying to maintain the same proportions, such as $8 on 7-8-39 and $5 on 3-8-39. (Note that I don't separate the 3/9 in the last race, since I like them equally.)

While much of this seems tedious, proper gambling strategy demands thinking long-run, rather than concerning yourself with merely cashing a ticket this afternoon.

Using this strategy, you will always be betting odd amounts ($17 on this combination, $9 on that one, $4 on another, etc.)—so do not use the betting cards provided by your track. Instead, write your numbers on a separate sheet along with the amounts you'll bet on each combination, and call them to the clerk.

Since you may be playing a dozen tickets using various combinations in differing amounts, bet early so you'll have plenty of time to check your tickets. Then, you can analyze the other possible bets in the first race in the pick 3. I usually wait for the first couple of flashes (to give me some indication of who might be overbet, or underbet, in the first part of the pick 3)—but I don't want to be stuck on line with two minutes to post, a dozen screaming strangers ahead of me, and an inexperienced clerk who keeps pressing "exacta part-wheel" on his machine when he should be pressing "pick 3 part-wheel."

Learn your local pick 3 terminology. You might call "$2 pick 3 part-wheel 4 and 357 and 239" at one track, and "$2 pick 3 part-wheel 4 with 3 and 5 and 7 with 2 and 3 and 9" at another.

Every pick 3 is different—and by making an odds line for each race, you'll be able to make out exactly the tickets that suit that day's play. Even if you don't make a line for a particular race in the pick 3, at least select which horses are your A's and which are your B's.

While generally your A horse should be your top pick, it doesn't necessarily have to be your most-likely-to-win selection. It could well be a third choice you think will be way underbet. The idea when making out the tickets is not just to cash—if all three of your top choices are 4-5 shots and they all win, the ticket will pay just about zero—but to benefit when an underbet horse comes in.

Below is a typical Pick 3 worksheet. Next to each horse's name is what percent chance I estimate he has to win. On this particular ticket I will insist that at least one of my circled top choices (Aaron, Doug, or the equal co-top choices of Fred and Gil) must win, so I pass up the ticket of 3-1-6 and 9-1-6. I also don't want them *all* to win or I'll get one of those all-favorite tickets that pay nothing, so I pass on 2-4-75.

Each of the nine tickets I then put in has a different percentage chance to win, which I determine by multiplying on my $5 calculator. Then I add the products of each to come up with today's chance of hitting, approximately 23.9%. I then decide how much I want to spend, then wager proportionally. If I decide to spend $239, for instance, I'd simply bet ten times the chances of each ticket ($28 on 2-4-6, $10 on 9-1-75, etc.).

Pick 3 Worksheet

1ST	② Aaron	.45
	3 Billy	.20
	9 Carl	.14

| 2ND | ④ Doug | .35 |
| | 1 Eddie | .28 |

3RD	⑦ Fred	.25
	⑤ Gil	.25
	6 Hal	.18

2 2 2 3 3 3 9 9 9 9

4 1 1 4 4 1 4 4 1

6 7 6 7 6 7 7 6 7
   5   5   5   5   5

2.8 3.1 2.2 1.7 1.2 1.4   1.2 0.9 1.0
     3.1   1.7   1.4   1.2   1.0

MULTIPLE WIN EXOTICS:
THE PICK 4 AND PICK 6

Multiple win exotics can turn a mediocre meeting into something memorable. They can also drive you to the loony bin, especially when you're alive for the whole pool into the last and get beat a nose.

Let's discuss the pick 4 first, and it will be a short discussion. This bet lies somewhere between the pick 3 (in which you bet odd amounts on various combinations, looking for value and hoping to hit the number several times) and the pick 6 (in which you look to hit the number once).

As with the pick 3, avoid putting in one large ticket combining everything with everything. Instead, insist that somebody must win—your top choice in leg 3, or one of your top two in leg 2, etc. Make out tickets that reflect how you feel about the particular pick 4, using the charts at the end of this chapter.

The rest of this section will discuss the pick 6, although much of what goes for the pick 6 is applicable to pick 4 betting, too.

The pick 6 began in 1980 at Hollywood Park and proved a big local hit. Results elsewhere have been mixed. The problem is simple—if fans don't bet enough money, nobody cares about the pick 6. A $5,000 pool attracts a lot less interest than a $500,000 pool.

In 1983 came a dramatic shift in the mathematics of pick 6 play with the introduction of the carryover concept (anywhere from half to three-quarters of the pool is carried over to the next day if no one hits all six winners). This switch from the pick 6 to the perfect 6 not only made the gimmick far more attractive on carryover days, but it also provided for a gambling rarity—a positive-expectation play, in that more money may be given out on a single afternoon than is taken in.

While the pick 6 was originally conceived as an anti-lottery scheme for the little guy, the big syndicates quickly moved in to crush and are still crushing at some tracks today. Perhaps the best example of this was the 1983 jai alai score by a group that bet $524,288 to play every possible combination after a fronton's carryover reached $551,331 after 45 days of bettor frustration. Against resources like this, the small player has scant chance.

Giant tickets are the order of the day at the nation's biggest tracks. Some groups think nothing of sending in a $10,000 sheet. This is risk-taking on a major scale, since the typical perfect 6 payoff is half that amount. A three-year, 256-day survey of the perfect 6 at Hollywood Park found the average payoff for six wins was $4,952 while the typical payoff for five was a mere $258. During the 30-day fall 1985 meeting at Holly-wood, the average return for a perfect 6 was a paltry $2,157—less than you could have earned on a decent exacta.

But though the tracks liked the extra action provided by the syndicates, they had two problems. First, the little players eventually recognized that they were merely cannon fodder for the guns of the big players, and they didn't like it. Second, the huge money to be won on carryover days was an invitation for cheating—and with trainers and jockeys joining syndicates (even if they used their own horses on their tickets), a scandal didn't appear far away.

As a result, Santa Anita eliminated the carryover, giving out the total pool every day and awarding consolations not only to those who had the second highest number of winners, but to those who had the third high-est as well (splitting the pot 60-20-20). From time to time that meant paying $2.80 to people with three winners, which may be stretching the idea of consolation payoffs a bit—and as 1988 began, Santa Anita switched to a no-carryover, 60-40 payout schedule.

The pick 6 without a carryover is far less attractive than a pick 6 with a carryover. But, either way, it's the possibility of a giant 6 that keeps the big players plunging and the little ones dreaming. Pools at the West-ern tracks have occasionally exceeded $2 million, and the pick 6 payoff often tops $100,000. Nearly one-fourth of the time at Santa Anita and

Hollywood, not a single ticket at the track has six winners—so one small change on a ticket may mean hundreds of thousands of dollars.

Though luck plays a major role in the pick 6—you go six deep in a race and your 4-5 top choice beats your 24-1 outsider by a nose, thereby reducing your payoff from $48,000 to $2,000 in a hurry—there are ways to maximize your chances while minimizing your risks.

And certainly the risks in pick 6 play are far greater than those in straight wagering. It's easy to lose 100 consecutive pick 6 plays. If you're betting tiny tickets, you could go to the track every day for a year and never hit, tossing away thousands of dollars in the process. If you're playing big tickets, you may be tempted to spend too high a percentage of your bankroll on the pick 6.

By joining a partner or partners on a ticket, you increase your chances of hitting without having to drastically raise the stakes. Better to have $200 of a $1000 winning ticket than to play your own $200 ticket which falls just short. The bigger the carryover, the more important it is to put in a major ticket. My own rule is never to play without a carryover, play with a $50,000 carryover only if I like the ticket, and play with a $100,000 carryover in all circumstances. On the day I hit the $114,446 pick six, the carryover exceeded $164,000.

Every time you play a pick 6, calculate your chances of winning. After making your lines, multiply:

```
1st —#5 (.45), #4 (.20), #7 (.15) ...................................3 (.80)
2nd—#1 (.50).........................................................1 (.50)
3rd—#6 (.30), #3 (.25), #1 (.15), #5 (.15) ..........................4 (.85)
4th—#2 (.60).........................................................1 (.60)
5th—#3 (.25), #4 (.25), #7 (.15), #9 (.12) ..........................4 (.77)
6th—#4 (.35), #1 (.20), #3 (.15).....................................3 (.70)
```

With $1 \times 1 \times 3 \times 3 \times 4 \times 4$, this ticket of 144 combinations would cost $288 and have an 11% chance of hitting six winners. A payoff of $2618 would break even. With a 50% bonus requirement, we'd need $3927. If I don't think it will pay that much, I won't play—at least not with this ticket.

How can I tell what the number might pay? I can't, but I can sometimes estimate the range. Let's say the entire pick 6 pool on a Wednesday at Obscure Downs is only $7,000 with the track distributing 50% of the net pool each day to those hitting all six winners. With a 25% takeout, the pool for those who sweep the six will be just $2625 (plus the same amount for holders of five)—meaning that even I have the only ticket at the track with six, I am making a play of no value.

Let's change locales to a Saturday at Big-League Park where the pick 6 pool totals $500,000, with 75% going to those with all six. Deducting the 25% state-track grab, we have $281,250 waiting to be won for all six, a decent amount. However, I then must calculate the approximate percentage of the pool that will be bet on each of my winners; I make two estimations—one with my longest shots winning, and one with my favorites. I assume the crowd will bet my horses in the percentage-of-win chance that I assign to these horses (although this is never exactly the case).

Let's assume all my top choices win and I could have had the whole thing for $2. According to my calculations, 885 tickets will have this winning combo, for a dismal payoff of $317—probably even worse, since many small players will have this number. On the up side, if all my longest-priced contenders win, I figure there will be just 30 winning tickets for a return of $9375. Under no circumstances will this ticket be worth $100,000.

There's quite a range between $317 and $9375. The midpoint of those two extremes is $4846, but since favorites win far more often than longshots, the pick 6 figures to fall far short of $4846—and below my requirements.

These calculations will be false to some extent because the public rarely goes for, for example, 60% of their pick 6 money on a single horse. It's possible that the horse I give a 50% win chance to will actually go off at 5-2, which would then make my ticket far more valuable. And I'm not including consolation payoffs for five winners in my calculations.

However, we're talking average—and for an average day with no carryover, I wouldn't play this ticket. But the picture changes dramatically with a $300,000 carryover in addition to that day's $281,250 net for all six. Now, each of those 885 winning favorite tickets would be worth $656, and each of the 30 winning longshot tickets would be worth $19,375. Averaging the extremes now yields a midpoint payoff of $10,015; if the number pays half this price, I'm getting value (remember that I needed only $3927 to make the play). So I put in the ticket.

The carryover is a key factor in deciding whether to play the pick 6. The higher the carryover, the more money you may be willing to risk, because selecting all six winners is crucial on the big carryover days when you have a chance to earn some real money. If anyone hits six, your ticket with five winners is virtually useless.

That's what ruins small players. Their tickets simply have too little chance of hitting all six winners. Someone playing a $32 or $64 ticket must use several favorites; if the ticket does come in, it probably won't pay much anyway. (How would you like to have hit six the day at Aqueduct when six winners returned $71 and the consolation for five winners was a mighty $3?) Better to take that $64 and get 10% of a decent ticket, or even 5% if the carryover is big enough.

While everyone has heard stories of the $2 player whose telephone number took down the whole pool, far more frequent is the tale of the $48 player who had four wins and took down zero. Those bets can add up over the cost of the meeting—and may, in fact, negate all your wins from other bets.

In the pick 6, *the little players simply become contributors to the positive cash flow of the big players.* While players compete equally in the win and exacta pools, the player who can afford to bet big has a huge edge in pick 6 competition. Not only does he have every horse the small player has, but he has many more—and if even one of those extras wins, the small player's ticket is dead, killed by the big player's.

And those winners don't have to be longshots, either. The small player must hone in on several races, trying desperately to get at least one (and possibly four) singles home. The syndicates, though, can afford to be wrong on every race and still hit the jackpot. A ticket of $2 \times 4 \times 4 \times 4 \times 5 \times 6$, for example, would run $7680—but on a day where every race looks open and the carryover is huge, such a ticket could be worth upwards of $200,000 even if nothing especially weird comes in. Little players cannot possibly have such coverage.

Big players can afford the luxury of throw-ins (as in, "He's got a small shot, throw him in."). And on a day when there does appear to be one standout single, the big players can really have fun. While the little guys are going $1 \times 2 \times 2 \times 2 \times 2 \times 3$ for $96, the syndicates are enjoying $1 \times 4 \times 4 \times 5 \times 6 \times 6$ for $5760. While the big players may lose money if the number comes back short, the little guy has almost no chance to take down that giant $175,000 payoff with his ticket—while the big guy does.

If you are a small player who can afford only $32 to play the pick 6, here are your options: skip the pick 6 altogether, play the $32 yourself and keep donating, or combine with other players on a group ticket.

The problem with group play, of course, is that everyone has an opinion. Joe wants a certain horse included that everyone else hates. Bill despises the single that Steve loves. Ernie wants to go five deep in the fifth while Ted thinks that's the race to use two horses at most. Better to have one expert handicapper make the final decisions, then give everyone a choice as to whether he wants to participate.

It's not enough merely to have six winners. You also have to beat the other couples. When a pick 6 looks like stealing because every race seems obvious, don't play—everybody at the track will be using the same few horses, and it's no big accomplishment to play an $864 ticket that returns $600.

One of the big decisions in making out a pick 6 is which horse to single. One school says single the most likely winner. Another says find a race where you have six or seven contenders and stab, since the big boys are using the whole bunch and this is your chance to even the odds. A third says look for a solid second or third choice to single, rather than a strong favorite that the whole world has.

Though I generally single my best horse, I find some problems with all three methods. If you and the entire track single the same 1-5 shot, the pick 6 may not pay much if it hits and you'll lose if the horse blows. If you stab among a bunch, you'll lose that race 80% of the time—and if you start with one race where you have just a 20% chance to win, imagine how slim your chances will be after you've gone through the rest of the card. If you single a solid 4-1 shot on a $768 card and someone else on your sheet misses, you've thrown away the $3840 you would have collected by merely betting that horse to win without any further risk.

I have seen scramble formulas (generally advertised with names like "The Genius Super Secret Pick Six Formula") that purportedly give you "$1536 worth of action for only $176." If you bet $176, or $32, or $16, on a ticket, that's what you get. You cannot cover every eventuality with a small ticket, no matter what the ads claim.

This does not mean, however, that your only option is one giant ticket. Far from it. In fact, I rarely put in one big ticket. I may give five horses in a race a chance, but usually I don't like them all equally—so why should I give them equal weight in my pick 6 play?

Every pick 6 is different. Some examples:
- 1 solid single; 3 races where two horses stand out; 2 races that look wide open
- 2 solid singles; 1 race in which three horses seem evenly matched; 3 races that look impossible
- No apparent single; 2 races in which three horses are contenders but one of the contenders stands way above the others; 4 races where several horses have a shot

You need a method that takes into account these varying types of pick 6's. One giant ticket won't do it.

Let's bring back the chart of a typical pick 6 from earlier in this chapter:

1st —#5 (.45), #4 (.20), #7 (.15) ....3 (.80)
2nd—#1 (.50)..1 (.50)
3rd—#6 (.30), #3 (.25), #1 (.15), #5 (.15) ....4 (.85)
4th—#2 (.60)..1 (.60)
5th—#3 (.25), #4 (.25), #7 (.15), #9 (.12) ....4 (.77)
6th—#4 (.35), #1 (.20), #3 (.15)....................................3 (.70)

One big ticket here would cost $288. In the first race, we like #5 three times as much as #7. In the sixth, we prefer #4 far above #3. To save money, we can make two tickets—one using our first-race choice as a single, and a second using our sixth race choice as a single. The tickets would be:

| 5 | 1 | 6315 | 2 | 3479 | 413 |
| 47 | 1 | 6315 | 2 | 3479 | 4 |

This cuts our cost to $160, a 45% reduction, while dropping our chances of winning by only 19% (the chance that both #5 in the first and #4 in the last will lose).

This method also probably cuts our chances of making a large score, since we're relying more heavily on the favorites to come in. However, it does reduce the outlay while maintaining a decent chance at a six.

Better, though, is a more sophisticated method that calls for playing *exactly the tickets that suit that day's card.* The charts at the end of this chapter indicate how many tickets you must make out, and how much these tickets cost, for any number of horses (up to six) in each race.

Let's say you've narrowed the card to 2-3-4-4-4-6. Not much narrowing, actually—no singles and a total cost of $4608. At this point, most players start eliminating their outside choices, or maybe stab for a single in a race they dislike.

There is an alternative, however. What if you leave in every contender and single nobody, but insist that at least two of your top choices—any two—win? How much would that cost and what kind of ticket would you need?

According to the charts, you'd have to make up 57 tickets at a cost of $2610. If you insist on three of your top choices winning, you could reduce your play to $1080 with 42 tickets. With four of your top choices winning, you'd need only $268 and 22 tickets.

These methods give you an opportunity at a large payoff, since you're leaving in your longshots rather than bumping them from the tickets to save money. But they do allow you to play for less money. While occasionally such a savings may be costly (as when none of your top choices win, or you need two out of a certain four and only one gets there), in the long run these types of tickets will enable you to have your best shot at big money while not putting in extravagant "throw-in" tickets.

With the charts, you can design tickets to suit the occasion. On some tickets, for example, your A horse could be your top three picks; in others, your A could be just your top choice. Some days you might spread equally in three races, then insist that at least one of your other three top choices wins.

Let's say, for instance, that you have three completely wide-open maiden races, and three other races in which you have an opinion. In the maiden races you have 4, 4, and 5 contenders. In the other races you have 2, 3, and 5. One giant ticket would cost $4800. But what if you decided to leave in every maiden contender but insisted that at least two of your top choices in the other three races win? A glance at the "three singles" chart (since using $4 \times 4 \times 5$ in three races is the same as using $1 \times 1 \times 1$, only 80 times more expensive) and some quick figuring shows that trims the cost to $1280.

Using these more sophisticated charts and formulas should put you far ahead of the typical pick 6 player, who either plays his birthday or who tries to make one big ticket with everything he likes, reluctantly having to cut nearly everyone but his top choices to get his ticket down to manageable size.

Once you get involved in a pick 6, don't daydream. Individual races may still offer value. It's silly to skip a 6-1 winner just because you figure you already have him on your ticket. Or pass up the overlaid favorite in the fifth race because he's your single and you're happy just to be alive.

On occasion, you will have to bet against a pick 6 selection. For example, you single the third event with a horse who's going off at 3-5. Your second choice in the race, whom you think is worth 4-1, is being let away at 9-1. Even though a victory by this 9-1 shot is going to eliminate your pick 6, play him to win.

Don't save. From time to time, you will be alive heading into the final race with two horses and be tempted to bet others. While it's true that such a plan will make you money for that race, in the long run it's a losing play.

You may at times send in more money on a horse than you had originally intended. Not only did you single him on your $432 ticket, but he looks like an overlay in the win, place, show, and exacta pools besides. Bet. Whether or not you played him in the pick 6 shouldn't influence what you do later. You are keeping a separate pick 6 bankroll, aren't you?

Handicap before you get to the track. Mark your tickets after late scratches, keeping the official program numbers handy. Attempting to analyze each race in the few minutes after you arrive at the track is foolish. Rushing to mark 25 cards, it's easy to make a mistake which could turn your $100,000 pick 6 into a $100 pick 5.

On the final day of a meeting when every dollar in the pool must by law be given out even if no one hits all six winners, always put in a ticket. And if the carryover is large, a giant sheet may be in order. On getaway day, hitting only five winners—usually no thrill at all—may bring you thousands of dollars. So be bold.

The charts are constructed on the model of our pick 3 charts in the last chapter. They assume that every horse will fall into one of the four groups described in that chapter (single, above-the-line top choice or choices, below-the-line contenders, and throwouts). Read them as you would the pick 3 charts.

Here's an example: You've narrowed a pick 6 to these contenders, with the A (top choice) listed first in each race:

Leg 1....................6	3	4	5	
Leg 2....................5				
Leg 3....................4	1	2	7	
Leg 4....................1	5			
Leg 5....................3				
Leg 6....................8	2	4	5	6

Your total combinations are $4 \times 1 \times 4 \times 2 \times 1 \times 5$. Looking under the chart for 2 singles, the combination "SS2445" costs \$320 ($160 \times \$2$).

Your two singles are #5 in the second leg of the pick 6 and #3 in the fifth leg. Your top non-singles are #6 in the first leg, #4 in the third, #1 in the fourth, and #8 in the sixth. If two of these top non-singles (which we refer to as "A" in the charts) win, you would need to invest only \$110 (55 combos as listed under 2A multiplied by \$2 per combination).

Turn to the chart that shows how to mark these tickets. You will fill out three divisions—4A (1 ticket), 3A (4 more tickets), and 2A (6 more tickets)—a total of 11 tickets.

The 11 tickets are listed on the next page.

I write all the numbers on a separate piece of paper, circling the A's for easy reference. Then I mark the singles first, since they will not change from card to card. Then I start with the first ticket—AAAASS —saying softly to myself, "A...A...A...A" (since the two S's have already been marked) and mark the tickets accordingly. Then it's on to "A...A...A...B" and so on until all the tickets have been marked.

The pick 6 gives us a shot at the kind of big money it might take years to accumulate from win betting. And despite the high takeout and the difficulty of bringing it down, the rewards make it worthwhile—assuming that your heart can survive those days when you're alive with six horses in the last and manage to miss for a six-figure turnaround.

The pick 6 may be tough to hit, but it's seldom boring. And it just might turn your life around.

But don't play the pick 6 just to have some action. The takeout is gigantic—a minimum of 20% every day, and a whopping 60% on the days that no one hits six (since half the available money is carried over to the next day). Assuming that 24% of the time there is a carryover (at small tracks the pool will carry over far more often, but it may take six straight days of misses to build a decent jackpot), that means the overall pick 6 takeout on non-carryover days is a huge 29.6%.

The only time to play the pick 9 is on the last day of the meeting when the track must give it all away. Tracks in California pay out a miniscule 30% of the Pick 9 pool when no hits all nine, carrying over the rest. Because it is virtually impossible to sweep all nine, a pick 9 player is bucking a 70% takeout. This is less than brilliant. When the track must give out all the money, the equation changes since the track is actually paying out more than it is taking in that day—a positive expectation play. Of course, there's always the chance that some syndicate will throw in a $50,000 sheet and hit all nine which nullifies your lousy eight—but who said you could gamble without some risk?

AAAASS

AAABSS   **AABASS**   **ABAASS**   **BAAASS**

BAABSS   **ABABSS**   **AABBSS**

BABASS   **ABBASS**   **BBAASS**

PICK 4

2 singles

2A (1 ticket)
1st... A
2nd...A
3rd... S
4th... S
———————
1A (2 more=3)
1st... A   B
2nd...B   A
3rd... S   S
4th... S   S
———————
0A (1 more=4)
1st... B
2nd...B
3rd... S
4th... S

	1A	0A
SS22	3	4
SS23	4	6
SS24	5	8
SS25	6	10
SS26	7	12
SS33	5	9
SS34	6	12
SS35	7	15
SS36	8	18
SS44	7	16
SS45	8	20
SS46	9	24
SS55	9	25
SS56	10	30
SS66	11	36

1 single

3A (1 ticket)
1st... A
2nd...A
3rd... A
4th... S
———————
2A (3 more=4)
1st... A   A   B
2nd...A   B   A
3rd... B   A   A
4th... S   S   S
———————
1A (3 more=7)
1st... A   B   B
2nd...B   A   B
3rd... B   B   A
4th... S   S   S
———————
0A (1 more=8)
1st... B
2nd...B
3rd... B
4th... S

	2A	1A	0A		2A	1A	0A
S222	4	7	8	S336	10	34	54
S223	5	10	12	S344	9	30	48
S224	6	13	16	S345	10	36	60
S225	7	16	20	S346	11	42	72
S226	8	20	24	S355	11	43	75
S233	6	14	18	S356	12	50	90
S234	7	18	24	S366	13	58	108
S235	8	22	30	S444	10	37	64
S236	9	26	36	S445	11	44	80
S244	8	23	32	S446	12	51	96
S245	9	28	40	S455	12	52	100
S246	10	33	48	S456	13	60	120
S255	10	34	50	S466	14	69	140
S256	11	40	60	S555	13	61	125
S266	12	47	72	S556	14	70	150
S333	7	19	27	S566	15	80	180
S334	8	24	36	S666	16	91	216
S335	9	29	45				

Pick 4 (no singles) appears on next page

PICK 4

0 singles

4A (1 ticket)
1st... A
2nd...A
3rd... A
4th... A

3A (4 more = 5)
1st... A A A B
2nd...A A B A
3rd... A B A A
4th... B A A A

2A (6 more = 11)
1st... B A A B A B
2nd...A B A A B B
3rd... A A B B B A
4th... B B B A A A

1A (4 more = 15)
1st... B B B A
2nd...B B A B
3rd... B A B B
4th... A B B B

0A (1 more = 16)
1st... B
2nd...B
3rd... B
4th... B

	3A	2A	1A	0A
2222	5	11	15	16
2223	6	15	22	24
2224	7	19	29	32
2225	8	23	36	40
2226	9	27	43	48
2233	7	20	32	36
2234	8	25	42	48
2235	9	30	52	60
2236	10	35	62	72
2244	9	31	55	64
2245	10	37	68	80
2246	11	43	81	96
2255	11	44	84	100
2256	12	51	100	120
2266	13	59	119	144
2333	8	26	46	54
2334	9	32	60	72
2335	10	38	74	90
2336	11	44	88	108
2344	10	39	78	96
2345	11	46	96	120
2346	12	53	114	144
2355	12	54	118	150
2356	13	62	140	180
2366	14	71	166	216
2444	11	47	101	128
2445	12	55	124	160
2446	13	63	147	192
2455	13	64	152	200
2456	14	73	180	240
2466	15	83	213	288
2555	14	74	186	250
2556	15	84	220	300
2566	16	95	260	360
2666	17	107	307	432

	3A	2A	1A	0A
3333	9	33	65	81
3334	10	40	84	108
3335	11	47	103	135
3336	12	54	122	162
3344	11	48	108	144
3345	12	56	132	180
3346	13	64	156	216
3355	13	65	161	225
3356	14	74	190	270
3366	15	84	224	324
3444	12	57	138	192
3445	13	66	168	240
3446	14	75	198	288
3455	14	76	204	300
3456	15	86	240	360
3466	16	97	282	432
3555	15	87	247	375
3556	16	98	290	450
3566	17	110	340	540
3666	18	123	398	648
4444	13	67	175	256
4445	14	77	212	320
4446	15	87	249	384
4455	15	88	256	400
4456	16	99	300	480
4466	17	111	351	576
4555	16	100	308	500
4556	17	112	360	600
4566	18	125	420	720
4666	19	139	489	864
5555	17	96	369	625
5556	18	126	430	750
5566	19	140	500	900
5666	20	155	580	1080
6666	21	171	671	1296

PICK 6

4 singles

2A (1 ticket)
1st... A
2nd...A
3rd... S
4th... S
5th... S
6th... S

1A (2 more = 3)
1st... A   B
2nd...B   A
3rd... S   S
4th... S   S
5th... S   S
6th... S   S

0A (1 more = 4)
1st... B
2nd...B
3rd... S
4th... S
5th... S
6th... S

	1A	0A
SSSS22	3	4
SSSS23	4	6
SSSS24	5	8
SSSS25	6	10
SSSS26	7	12
SSSS33	5	9
SSSS34	6	12
SSSS35	7	15
SSSS36	8	18
SSSS44	7	16
SSSS45	8	20
SSSS46	9	24
SSSS55	9	25
SSSS56	10	30
SSSS66	11	36

Pick 6 (3 singles) appears on next page

PICK 6

3 singles

3A (1 ticket)			
1st... A			
2nd...A			
3rd... A			
4th... S			
5th... S			
6th... S			

2A (3 more = 4)			
1st... A	A	B	
2nd...A	B	A	
3rd... B	A	A	
4th... S	S	S	
5th... S	S	S	
6th... S	S	S	

1A (3 more = 7)			
1st... A	B	B	
2nd...B	A	B	
3rd... B	B	A	
4th... S	S	S	
5th... S	S	S	
6th... S	S	S	

0A (1 more = 8)			
1st... B			
2nd...B			
3rd... B			
4th... S			
5th... S			
6th... S			

	2A	1A	0A
SSS222	4	7	8
SSS223	5	10	12
SSS224	6	13	16
SSS225	7	16	20
SSS226	8	20	24
SSS233	6	14	18
SSS234	7	18	24
SSS235	8	22	30
SSS236	9	26	36
SSS244	8	23	32
SSS245	9	28	40
SSS246	10	33	48
SSS255	10	34	50
SSS256	11	40	60
SSS266	12	47	72
SSS333	7	19	27
SSS334	8	24	36
SSS335	9	29	45
SSS336	10	34	54
SSS344	9	30	48
SSS345	10	36	60
SSS346	11	42	72
SSS355	11	43	75
SSS356	12	50	90
SSS366	13	58	108
SSS444	10	37	64
SSS445	11	44	80
SSS446	12	51	96
SSS455	12	52	100
SSS456	13	60	120
SSS466	14	69	140
SSS555	13	61	125
SSS556	14	70	150
SSS566	15	80	180
SSS666	16	91	216

Pick 6 (2 singles) appears on next page

PICK 6

2 singles

4A (1 ticket)
1st... A
2nd...A
3rd... A
4th... A
5th... S
6th... S

3A (4 more = 5)
1st... A A A B
2nd...A A B A
3rd... A B A A
4th... B A A A
5th... S S S S
6th... S S S S

2A (6 more = 11)
1st... B A A B A B
2nd...A B A A B B
3rd... A A B B B A
4th... B B B A A A
5th... S S S S S S
6th... S S S S S S

1A (4 more = 15)
1st... B B B A
2nd...B B A B
3rd... B A B B
4th... A B B B
5th... S S S S
6th... S S S S

0A (1 more = 16)
1st... B
2nd...B
3rd... B
4th... B
5th... S
6th... S

	3A	2A	1A	0A		3A	2A	1A	0A
SS2222	5	11	15	16	SS3333	9	33	65	81
SS2223	6	15	22	24	SS3334	10	40	84	108
SS2224	7	19	29	32	SS3335	11	47	103	135
SS2225	8	23	36	40	SS3336	12	54	122	162
SS2226	9	27	43	48	SS3344	11	48	108	144
SS2233	7	20	32	36	SS3345	12	56	132	180
SS2234	8	25	42	48	SS3346	13	64	156	216
SS2235	9	30	52	60	SS3355	13	65	161	225
SS2236	10	35	62	72	SS3356	14	74	190	270
SS2244	9	31	55	64	SS3366	15	84	224	324
SS2245	10	37	68	80	SS3444	12	57	138	192
SS2246	11	43	81	96	SS3445	13	66	168	240
SS2255	11	44	84	100	SS3446	14	75	198	288
SS2256	12	51	100	120	SS3455	14	76	204	300
SS2266	13	59	119	144	SS3456	15	86	240	360
SS2333	8	26	46	54	SS3466	16	97	282	432
SS2334	9	32	60	72	SS3555	15	87	247	375
SS2335	10	38	74	90	SS3556	16	98	290	450
SS2336	11	44	88	108	SS3566	17	110	340	540
SS2344	10	39	78	96	SS3666	18	123	398	648
SS2345	11	46	96	120	SS4444	13	67	175	256
SS2346	12	53	114	144	SS4445	14	77	212	320
SS2355	12	54	118	150	SS4446	15	87	249	384
SS2356	13	62	140	180	SS4455	15	88	256	400
SS2366	14	71	166	216	SS4456	16	99	300	480
SS2444	11	47	101	128	SS4466	17	111	351	576
SS2445	12	55	124	160	SS4555	16	100	308	500
SS2446	13	63	147	192	SS4556	17	112	360	600
SS2455	13	64	152	200	SS4566	18	125	420	720
SS2456	14	73	180	240	SS4666	19	139	489	864
SS2466	15	83	213	288	SS5555	17	96	369	625
SS2555	14	74	186	250	SS5556	18	126	430	750
SS2556	15	84	220	300	SS5566	19	140	500	900
SS2566	16	95	260	360	SS5666	20	155	580	1080
SS2666	17	107	307	432	SS6666	21	171	671	1296

Pick 6 (1 single) appears on next page

PICK 6

1 single

```
5A (1 ticket)
1st... A
2nd...A
3rd... A
4th... A
5th... A
6th... S
```

```
4A (5 more = 6)
1st... A  A  A  A  B
2nd...A  A  A  B  A
3rd... A  A  B  A  A
4th... A  B  A  A  A
5th... B  A  A  A  A
6th... S  S  S  S  S
```

```
3A (10 more = 16)
1st... B  A  A  A  B  A  A  B  A  B
2nd...A  B  A  A  A  B  A  A  B  B
3rd... A  A  B  A  A  A  B  B  B  A
4th... A  A  A  B  B  B  B  A  A  A
5th... B  B  B  B  A  A  A  A  A  A
6th... S  S  S  S  S  S  S  S  S  S
```

```
2A (10 more = 26)
1st... B  B  B  A  A  A  B  B  A  B
2nd...B  A  A  B  B  A  B  A  B  B
3rd... A  B  A  B  A  B  A  B  B  B
4th... A  A  B  A  B  B  B  B  B  A
5th... B  B  B  B  B  B  A  A  A  A
6th... S  S  S  S  S  S  S  S  S  S
```

```
1A (5 more = 31)
1st... A  B  B  B  B
2nd...B  A  B  B  B
3rd... B  B  A  B  B
4th... B  B  B  A  B
5th... B  B  B  B  A
6th... S  S  S  S  S
```

```
0A (1 more = 32)
1st... B
2nd...B
3rd... B
4th... B
5th... B
6th... S
```

See next page for Pick 6 (1 single) combinations required

PICK 6

1 single

	4A	3A	2A	1A	0A
S22222	6	16	26	31	32
S22223	7	21	37	46	48
S22224	8	26	48	61	64
SS2225	9	31	59	76	80
S22226	10	36	70	91	96
S22233	8	27	52	68	72
S22234	9	33	67	90	96
S22235	10	39	82	112	120
S22236	11	45	97	134	144
S22244	10	40	86	119	128
S22245	11	47	105	148	160
S22246	12	54	124	177	192
S22255	12	55	128	184	200
S22256	13	63	151	220	240
S22266	14	72	178	263	288
S22333	9	34	72	100	108
S22334	10	41	92	132	144
S22335	11	46	112	164	180
S22336	12	55	132	196	216
S22344	11	49	117	174	192
S22345	12	57	142	216	240
S22346	13	65	167	258	288
S22355	13	66	172	268	300
S22356	14	75	202	320	360
S22366	15	85	237	382	432
S22444	12	58	148	229	256
S22445	13	67	179	284	320
S22446	14	76	210	339	384
S22455	14	77	216	352	400
S22456	15	87	253	420	480
S22466	16	98	296	501	576
S22555	15	88	260	436	500
S22556	16	99	304	520	600
S22566	17	111	355	620	720
S22666	18	124	414	739	864
S23333	10	42	98	146	162
S23334	11	50	124	192	216
S23335	12	58	150	238	270
S23336	13	66	176	284	324
S23344	12	59	156	252	288
S23345	13	68	188	312	360
S23346	14	77	220	372	432
S23355	14	78	226	386	450
S23356	15	88	264	460	540
S23366	16	99	308	548	648
S23444	13	69	195	330	384
S23445	14	79	234	408	480
S23446	15	89	273	486	576
S23455	15	90	280	504	600
S23456	16	101	326	600	720
S23466	17	113	379	714	864
S23555	16	102	334	622	750
S23556	17	114	388	740	900
S23566	18	127	450	880	1080
S23666	19	141	521	1046	1296
S24444	14	80	242	431	512
S24445	15	91	289	532	640
S24446	16	102	336	633	768
S24455	16	103	344	656	800
S24456	17	115	399	780	960
S24466	18	128	462	927	1152
S24555	17	116	408	808	1000
S24556	18	129	472	960	1200

	4A	3A	2A	1A	0A
S24566	19	143	545	1140	1440
S24666	20	158	628	1353	1728
S25555	18	130	482	994	1250
S25556	19	144	556	1180	1500
S25566	20	159	640	1400	1800
S25666	21	175	735	1660	2160
S26666	22	192	842	1967	2592
S33333	11	51	131	211	243
S33334	12	60	164	276	324
S33335	13	69	197	341	405
S33336	14	78	230	406	486
S33344	13	70	204	360	432
S33345	14	80	244	444	540
S33346	15	90	284	528	648
S33355	15	91	291	547	675
S33356	16	102	338	650	810
S33366	17	114	392	772	972
S33444	14	81	252	468	576
S33445	15	92	296	576	720
S33446	16	103	340	684	864
S33455	16	104	356	708	900
S33456	17	116	408	840	1080
S33466	18	129	476	1146	1296
S33555	17	117	437	869	1125
S33556	18	130	486	1030	1350
S33566	19	144	560	1220	1620
S33666	20	159	644	1444	1944
S34444	15	93	309	606	768
S34445	16	105	366	744	960
S34446	17	117	423	882	1152
S34455	17	118	432	912	1200
S34456	18	131	498	1080	1440
S34466	19	145	573	1278	1728
S34555	18	132	508	1116	1500
S34556	19	146	576	1320	1800
S34566	20	161	670	1560	2160
S34666	21	177	767	1842	2592
S35555	19	147	595	1363	1875
S35556	20	162	682	1610	2250
S35566	21	178	780	1900	2700
S35666	22	195	890	2240	3240
S36666	23	213	1013	2638	3888
S44444	16	106	376	781	1024
S44445	17	119	443	956	1280
S44446	18	132	510	1131	1536
S44455	18	133	520	1168	1600
S44456	19	147	597	1380	1920
S44466	20	162	684	1629	2304
S44555	19	148	608	1424	2000
S44556	20	163	696	1680	2400
S44566	21	179	795	1980	2880
S44666	22	196	906	2331	3450
S45555	20	164	708	1732	2500
S45556	21	180	808	2040	3000
S45566	22	197	920	1400	3600
S45666	23	215	1045	2820	4320
S46666	24	234	1184	3309	5184
S55555	21	181	821	2101	3125
S55556	22	198	934	2470	3750
S55566	23	216	1060	2900	4500
S55666	24	235	1220	3400	5400
S56666	25	255	1355	3980	6480
S66666	26	276	1526	4651	7776

PICK 6
0 singles

6A (1 ticket)
1st... A
2nd...A
3rd... A
4th... A
5th... A
6th... A

5A (6 more = 7)
1st... A A A A A B
2nd...A A A A B A
3rd...A A A B A A
4th...A A B A A A
5th...A B A A A A
6th...B A A A A A

4A (15 more = 22)
1st... B A A A A B A A A B A A B A B
2nd...A B A A A A B A A A B A A B B
3rd...A A B A A A A B A A A B B B A
4th...A A A B A A A A B B B B A A A
5th...A A A A B B B B B A A A A A A
6th...B B B B B A A A A A A A A A A

3A (20 more = 42)
1st... B A A A B A A B A B B B B A A A B B A B
2nd...A B A A A B A A B B B A A B B A B A B B
3rd...A A B A A A B B B A A B A B A B A B B B
4th...A A A B B B B A A A A A B A B B B B B A
5th...B B B B A A A A A A B B B B B B A A A A
6th...B B B B B B B B B B A A A A A A A A A A

2A (15 more = 57)
1st... B B B A A A B A B B B B B A B
2nd...B A A B B A B A B B B B A B B
3rd...A B A B A B A B B B B A B B B
4th...A A B A B B B B B A A B B B B
5th...B B B B B B A A A A B B B B A
6th...B B B B B B B B B B A A A A A

1A (6 more = 63)
1st... A B B B B B
2nd...B A B B B B
3rd... B B A B B B
4th... B B B A B B
5th... B B B B A B
6th... B B B B B A

0A (1 more = 64)
1st... B
2nd...B
3rd... B
4th... B
5th... B
6th... B

See next page for Pick 6 (0 singles) combinations required

PICK 6

0 singles

Note: If 10,000 or more combos are required, number will say 999*

	5A	4A	3A	2A	1A	0A
222222	7	22	42	57	63	64
222223	8	28	58	83	94	96
222224	9	34	74	109	125	128
222225	10	40	90	135	156	160
222226	11	46	106	161	187	192
222233	9	35	79	120	140	144
222234	10	42	100	157	186	192
222235	11	49	121	194	232	240
222236	12	56	142	231	278	288
222244	11	50	126	205	247	256
222245	12	58	152	253	308	320
222246	13	66	178	301	369	384
222255	13	67	183	312	384	400
222256	14	76	214	371	460	480
222266	15	86	250	441	551	576
222333	10	43	106	172	208	216
222334	11	51	133	224	276	288
222335	12	59	160	276	344	360
222336	13	67	187	328	412	432
222344	12	60	166	291	366	384
222345	13	69	199	358	456	460
222346	14	78	232	425	546	576
222355	14	79	238	440	568	600
222356	15	89	277	522	680	720
222366	16	100	322	619	814	864
222444	13	70	206	377	485	512
222445	14	80	246	463	604	640
222446	15	90	286	549	723	768
222455	15	91	293	568	752	800
222456	16	102	340	673	900	960
222466	17	114	394	797	1077	1152
222555	16	103	348	696	936	1000
222556	17	115	403	824	1120	1200
222566	18	128	466	975	1340	1440
222666	19	142	538	1153	1603	1728
223333	11	52	140	244	308	324
223334	12	61	174	316	408	432
223335	13	70	208	388	508	540
223336	14	79	242	460	608	648
223344	13	71	215	408	540	576
223345	14	81	256	500	672	720
223346	15	91	297	592	804	864
223355	15	92	304	612	836	900
223356	16	103	352	724	1000	1080
223366	17	115	407	856	1196	1296
223444	14	82	264	525	714	768
223445	15	93	313	642	888	960
223446	16	104	362	759	1062	1152
223455	16	105	370	784	1104	1200
223456	17	117	427	926	1320	1440
223466	18	130	492	1093	1578	1728
223555	17	118	436	956	1372	1500
223556	18	131	502	1128	1640	1800

	5A	4A	3A	2A	1A	0A
223566	19	145	577	1338	1850	2160
223666	20	160	662	1567	2342	2592
224444	15	94	322	673	943	1024
224445	16	106	380	821	1172	1280
224446	17	118	438	969	1401	1536
224455	17	119	447	1000	1456	1600
224456	18	132	514	1179	1740	1920
224466	19	146	590	1389	2079	2304
224555	18	133	524	1216	1808	2000
224556	19	147	601	1432	2160	2400
224566	20	162	688	1685	2580	2880
224666	21	178	786	1981	3081	3450
225555	19	148	612	1476	2244	2500
225556	20	163	700	1736	2680	3000
225566	21	179	799	2040	3200	3600
225666	22	196	910	2395	3820	4320
226666	23	214	1034	2809	4559	5180
233333	12	62	182	342	454	480
233334	13	72	224	440	600	648
233335	14	82	266	538	746	810
233336	15	92	308	636	892	972
233344	14	83	274	564	792	864
233345	15	94	324	688	984	1080
233346	16	105	374	812	1176	1296
233355	16	106	382	838	1222	1350
233356	17	118	440	988	1460	1620
233366	18	131	506	1164	1744	1944
233444	15	95	333	720	1044	1152
233445	16	107	392	876	1296	1440
233446	17	119	451	1032	1548	1728
233455	17	120	460	1064	1608	1800
233456	18	133	528	1252	1920	2160
233466	19	147	605	1472	2292	2592
233555	18	134	538	1290	1994	2250
233556	19	148	616	1516	2380	2700
233566	20	163	704	1780	2840	3240
233666	21	179	803	2088	3388	3888
234444	16	108	402	915	1374	1536
234445	17	121	471	1110	1704	1920
234446	18	134	540	1305	2034	2304
234455	18	135	550	1344	2112	2400
234456	19	149	629	1578	2520	2880
234466	20	164	718	1851	3006	3456
234555	19	150	640	1624	2616	3000
234556	20	165	730	1904	3120	3600
234566	21	181	831	2230	3720	4320
234666	22	198	944	2609	4434	5184
235555	20	166	742	1958	3238	3750
235556	21	182	844	2292	3860	4500
235566	22	199	958	2680	4600	5400
235666	23	217	1085	3130	4955	6480
236666	24	236	1226	3651	6526	7776
244444	17	122	482	1157	1805	2048

(continued on next page)

PICK 6

0 singles *(continued)*

	5A	4A	3A	2A	1A	0A
244445	18	136	562	1399	2236	2560
244446	19	150	642	1641	2667	3072
244455	19	151	653	1688	2768	3200
244456	20	166	744	1977	3300	3840
244466	21	182	846	2313	3933	4608
244555	20	167	756	2032	3424	4000
244556	21	183	859	2376	4080	4800
244566	22	200	974	2775	4860	5760
244666	23	218	1102	3237	5787	6912
245555	21	184	872	2440	4232	5000
245556	22	201	988	2848	5040	6000
245566	23	219	1117	3320	6000	7200
245666	24	238	1260	3865	7140	8440
246666	25	258	1418	4493	8493	999*
255555	22	202	1002	2922	5226	6250
255556	23	220	1132	3404	6220	7500
255566	24	239	1276	3960	7400	9000
255666	25	259	1435	4600	8800	999*
256666	26	280	1610	5335	999*	999*
266666	27	302	1802	6177	999*	999*
333333	13	73	233	473	665	729
333334	14	84	284	604	876	972
333335	15	95	335	735	1087	1215
333336	16	106	386	866	1298	1458
333344	15	96	344	768	1152	1296
333345	16	108	404	932	1428	1620
333346	17	120	464	1096	1704	1944
333355	17	121	473	1129	1769	2025
333356	18	134	542	1326	2110	2430
333366	19	148	620	1556	2516	2916
333444	16	109	414	972	1512	1728
333445	17	122	484	1176	1872	2160
333446	18	135	554	1380	2232	2592
333455	18	136	564	1420	2316	2700
333456	19	150	644	1664	2760	3240
333466	20	165	734	1948	3288	3888
333555	19	151	655	1711	2863	3375
333556	20	166	746	2002	3410	4050
333566	21	182	848	2340	4060	4860
333666	22	199	962	2732	4832	5832
334444	17	123	495	1224	1980	2304
334445	18	137	576	1476	2448	2880
334446	19	151	657	1728	2916	3456
334455	19	152	668	1776	3024	3600
334456	20	167	760	2076	3600	4332
334466	21	183	863	2424	4284	5184
334555	20	168	772	2132	3732	4500
334556	21	184	876	2488	4440	5400
334566	22	201	992	2900	5280	6480
334666	23	219	1121	3376	6276	7776
335555	21	185	889	2553	4601	5625
335556	22	202	1006	2974	5470	6750
335566	23	220	1136	3460	6500	8100
335666	24	239	1280	4020	7720	9720
336666	25	259	1439	4664	9164	999*
344444	18	138	588	1533	2586	3072
344445	19	153	681	1842	3192	3840
344446	20	168	774	2151	3798	4608
344455	20	169	786	2208	3936	4800
344456	21	185	891	2574	4680	5760
344466	22	202	1008	2997	5562	6912
344555	21	186	904	2640	4848	6000
344556	22	203	1022	3072	5760	7200
344566	23	221	1153	3570	6840	8640
344666	24	240	1298	4143	8118	999*
345555	22	204	1036	3148	5964	7500
345556	23	222	1168	3656	7080	9000
345566	24	241	1314	4240	8400	999*
345666	25	261	1475	4910	9960	999*
346666	26	282	1652	5677	999*	999*
355555	23	223	1183	3743	7327	9375
355556	24	242	1330	4338	8690	999*
355566	25	262	1492	5020	999*	999*
355666	26	283	1670	5800	999*	999*
356666	27	305	1865	6690	999*	999*
366666	28	328	2078	7703	999*	999*
444444	19	154	694	1909	3367	4096
444445	20	170	800	2285	4148	5120
444446	21	186	906	2661	4929	6144
444455	21	187	919	2728	5104	6400
444456	22	204	1038	3171	6060	7680
444466	23	222	1170	3681	7191	9616
444555	22	205	1052	3248	6272	8000
444556	23	223	1185	3768	7440	9600
444566	24	242	1332	4365	8820	999*
444666	25	262	1494	5049	999*	999*
445555	23	224	1200	3856	7696	999*
445556	24	243	1348	4464	9120	999*
445566	25	263	1511	5160	999*	999*
445666	26	284	1690	5955	999*	999*
446666	27	306	1886	6861	999*	999*
455555	24	244	1364	4564	9428	999*
455556	25	264	1528	5272	999*	999*
455566	26	285	1708	6080	999*	999*
455666	27	307	1905	7000	999*	999*
456666	28	330	2120	8045	999*	999*
466666	29	354	2354	9229	999*	999*
555555	25	265	1545	5385	999*	999*
555556	26	286	1726	6206	999*	999*
555566	27	308	1924	7140	999*	999*
555666	28	331	2140	8200	999*	999*
556666	29	355	2375	9400	999*	999*
566666	30	380	2630	999*	999*	999*
666666	31	406	2906	999*	999*	999*

A BETTING EDGE

Once you've determined how much to bet, there remains just one task —the physical act of betting.

Twenty years ago, you had to get on several lines for different bets— $10 win on one line, $5 place on another, $2 exactas on a third. That's all changed. Now virtually every major track has cash-sell machines where you can bet any amount at any window. Depending on the location, at a few places you can bet using a self-activated machine, at some you can bet at a satellite track or an off-track betting parlor, at others you can play by phone from the comfort of your living room.

From the professional standpoint, these are the most important considerations:
- How late can you bet without being shut out?
- Can you see exacta prices, win prices, and place and show pools up to the last moment?
- At harness races, can you bet on the bell?

In the ideal world, you could type your bets on a private screen, adjusting them with a simple keystroke up until seconds before off time, then press "yes" or "no" just before the field left the gate. In the real world, things are much tougher.

Every bettor has experienced the disaster of being shut out on a bet that could have made his season, or at least his night. As capital punishment is not permitted for those slowpokes who insist on handicapping a race just as they step up to the window, shutouts will probably always be with us.

You can avoid shutouts by betting early, of course, but our entire method is based on betting for value—and if you don't know the closing odds, you can't tell if the crowd is offering enough value. At most tracks, a large percentage of the money is bet in the last five minutes, and it's not unusual to see a fat 5-1 overlay at three minutes to post disappear to a useless 2-1 by off time. At small tracks, a single bet can wipe out what seemed to be a good overlay.

So you must bet late—as late as possible. Still, you must be able to see the changing mutuel pools and possible payoffs. A track with a wide-awake management that didn't mind spending a dollar would have television monitors over every mutuel window. Window #1 would have the win odds, #2 the place and show pools via a panning camera, and #3 the up-to-the-second changing exacta odds. In this way, you could wait on line and still see every payoff.

But few tracks offer anything this complete. At the typical track, win odds are in one spot, exacta odds in another, and the only way to see the place and show pools is by walking outside to study the toteboard. So we must compromise.

Since most of your bets will be in the win and exacta pools, *find a spot —on line—where you can see both pools.* At some tracks, TV monitors offer exactas while a large board near the mutuel windows shows the win odds. Other tracks show win odds and exacta prices on side-by-side, or nearby, monitors.

Whatever your track does, you must be able to get in line early enough to avoid a shutout, yet late enough to adjust your play at the last moment. If the grandstand windows are understaffed while the turf-club windows never have lines, it's worth paying the extra tariff to avoid shutouts.

Begin studying the monitors about six minutes to post time from a vantage point near the windows, so if a huge line suddenly appears for a race you can join it. In front of the monitors, circle any overlaid exacta combinations and check the win odds of each contender. Stroll outside to see the place and show pools. Before you get on line, you should know which bets you'll be considering—and they should all be marked on one sheet (I use the bottom of my exacta sheet) so you won't have to flip through several pages when you reach the window.

In this example race, we've made the following line:

#1	30-1	#6	30-1
#2	7-5	#7	8-1
#3	15-1	#8	100-1
#4	50-1	#9	50-1
#5	3-1	#10	25-1

At the six-minute mark, #2 is 2-1 and #5 is 5-2. It's unlikely that #5 will drift up to the 9-2 mark we need, so we don't pay much heed to his win odds any longer. The maximum permitted place-show numbers for #5 were 13.47 and 11.99, but he has nearly 20% of each pool, far too high.

With #5 having little chance of being a win overlay, we write the possible bets for #2. If he winds up at 2-1 when we bet, we'll play him for $30. At 5-2, we'll bet $32.

The favorite also is close to the cutoff points for a place and show bet. We need no more than 22.45% of the place pool, and as we check the pool just before getting on line he has 24%, just over the mark. To show our cutoff point is 19.99%, and #2 has only 18% to show. Although our maximum show bet for a 7-5 shot is $60, we calculate that a bet of $40 is all we can play without tipping him over the cutoff edge.

The circled exactas are 2-7, 7-2, and 7-5. Even after subtracting $4, they'd all be playable. Since we needed just $37 for a $3 bet on 2-7, we give an extra dollar for the extra value and tentatively mark $4 in the exacta square. We decide to play $3 on 7-2 and $2 on 7-5.

About three minutes to post (or five minutes to off time), we get in line. From our spot on the line, we continue to observe the win and exacta odds as the line snakes forward. If the line is short, we may be able to jump out and see the place and show pools at close to post time, for our final decision on those slots.

Note that as we get close to making our bet, we still may make last-second adjustments—not because the guy in front of us just bet $500 on a horse we hate, but because the odds are always changing. It's possible that #2 will dip to 9-5, too short to play to win. Or he won't get much further place action, which will drop him back below 22.45%.

Be prepared for last-second changes. For example, let's say we've got two apparent overlays—a horse we make 3-1 is listed at 5-1 and another we've tabbed at 6-1 is on the board at 10-1. It's possible that we'll bet one,

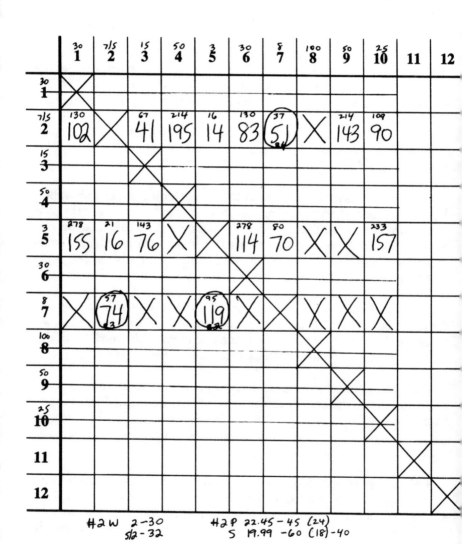

	30 1	7/5 2	15 3	50 4	3 5	30 6	8 7	100 8	50 9	25 10	11	12
30 1	✕											
7/5 2	130 102	✕	67 41	214 195	16 14	130 83	37 51	✕	214 143	109 90		
15 3												
50 4												
3 5	278 155	21 16	143 76	✕	✕	278 114	80 70	✕	✕	233 157		
30 6												
8 7	✕	57 74	✕	✕	95 119	✕	✕	✕	✕	✕		
100 8												
50 9												
25 10												
11												
12												

#2W 2-30
    s/2-32

#2P 22.45-45 (24)
    S 19.99 -60 (18)-40

both, or neither, depending on their final odds. On our exacta sheet, we may have seven combinations circled with two minutes to post—but late changes may make four of them unplayable, and perhaps another combination we didn't originally circle will emerge as an overlay.

Permit others behind you to move ahead—one at a time. In this way, you don't lose your place and you can bet just before the horses leave the gate. With practice, you'll be able to bet virtually at post time.

This strategy ensures that rarely will you be shut out, yet you'll be able to see the latest available odds. Of course another odds change comes just after the race begins, so a horse you needed 4-1 for may slip to 7-2, or an exacta you played at $42 may have dipped to $37.

Sometimes, lines are short. Maybe a cheap maiden claimer attracts little interest, or it's the final race and half the crowd has already left. At the harness races, that means a possible *bell-bet*.

Bell-betting is a giant edge that's possible at some harness tracks. To bell, you need three requirements:
- No one else on line
- A clear view of the race's start
- An efficient mutuel clerk

Let's say you're considering a horse from the seven post who could win, but only if he leaves. Seconds before post, tell the clerk, "Bet $100 to win on the 7 and lock it in." The clerk punches in your bet but does not press the button which would issue the ticket. Then, checking a nearby TV for the race's start, make sure your horse is coming to the gate as if the driver is going to leave. At the moment the race begins, you'll have a split second to shout "Yes" if you want the ticket to be issued. If it looks as though the horse is coming slowly to the gate as if the driver is planning to take back at the start, just walk away.

You and the teller must work as an efficient team. If you wait too long, you'll be shut out since the machines automatically lock just after the race starts. Call too early and you may be backing a non-leaver. You may also use this technique with the betting machines, pressing the "Print" button if the horse appears to be leaving.

When you have a contender who frequently breaks before the race, hover around the windows for a possible edge even if you hadn't thought of betting previously. You may be able to bet against a breaker. One night

I made two horses 2-1 on my line and that's what the crowd had them at, so I wasn't planning to play. However, one of them was a habitual breaker so I stayed close to the windows, just in case. Sure enough, just after the recall pole this horse jumped off stride—so I quickly called a $200 bet on the other horse, a sudden overlay since his main competition had been eliminated. I made nearly $500 on the race solely because I had been prepared.

If your horse causes a recall for breaking before the start, cancel your tickets on him; though occasionally these horses go on to win, in the long run you're better off passing them. The same is true for thoroughbreds that break through the gate before the official start, and for quarterhorses that appear skittish coming to the gate. (Some tracks, though, won't permit bet cancellations; try to wait until the last possible second to play at these stone-age institutions.)

At tracks where you can't see one or more of the pools, consider team betting. Jack waits on line (letting one player behind him pass at a time, of course) while Fred studies the appropriate pool or pools. At the last moment, Fred dashes from his vantage point at the last moment to notify Jack of any overlays.

Call your numbers clearly. Otherwise "$20 win 8" could be heard as "$20 1-8." And call them slowly enough for the teller to punch in your numbers without rushing, especially when you've got odd-sized bets or several exotic combinations. For instance, if you call a $55 exacta bet, the clerk may have to punch twice—$50 exacta and $5 exacta—so take your time to minimize errors.

Check your tickets. There's a perverse rule here—a clerk never seems to goof in your favor. As you call your bet, watch the teller's fingers to be sure he's pressing the right buttons. But mistakes do happen. By checking your tickets before you leave the window (even if you just stay off to the side to allow someone behind you to bet), you'll avoid problems. On a cold December day in 1985 at Kentucky's Turfway Park, somebody hit a pick 6 ticket for $77,434.80 but never cashed it. Two years later it was turned over to the state. Apparently, the owner had never bothered to check his ticket.

Other than inter-track betting (which is not as good as on-track betting, since you can't inspect the horses in the paddock or watch their warmups), I can't recommend playing off-track. You often have no access to the late odds, which is our number-one determinant of how much to play on what horse. And if you bet early, you may miss crucial late scratches or jockey changes.

If you must bet off-track, avoid places where you must pay a surcharge on winning bets. This tax may easily wipe out all your profits. In some jurisdictions you can avoid such a grab by keeping a minimum amount such as $500 in a telephone account, or by betting in teletheaters.

A better bet off-track is Nevada, where you can watch races live without having your bet affect the odds. Throw in free parking, admission, drinks, and a program, and your daily expenses are reduced to zero. However, you can't see late exacta prices and your payoffs may be limited —some race books pay full track odds only up to the first $20 bet (with a ceiling of 15-1 win, 6-1 place, and 3-1 show thereafter), while others limit exacta payoffs to as little as 100-1. While a casino will gladly accept a $10,000 sports bet, don't expect to bet $1,000 (at some books, as little as $100) on an 8-1 shot at Monmouth—even the biggest books won't take your bet (their euphemism for this is "limiting our exposure").

If your opinion is no good, you're not going to win no matter how you bet—but as a serious player with a winning edge, don't blow it by messing up your betting.

A DAY AT SANTA ANITA

On November 7, 1987, I ventured to Santa Anita with an expert thoroughbred handicapper, James Quinn. Not only is he the author of a number of books on racing, but he puts serious money through the windows.

Usually, Quinn doesn't compile a precise odds line. While he bets only when he feels he's getting overlay value—which is, of course, the essence of successful racetrack betting—Quinn prefers to do it more by feel than by numerical calculations. Nonetheless, as a favor to me, he gamely tried.

The first playable race turned out to be the first race on the card, an $18,000-$20,000 claimer. Quinn narrowed the race to three contenders, and made up this line (Q is Quinn's line, C is the crowd's line):

	Q	C
#6 And Justice	2-1	4-1
#1 Fond O' Green	3-1	8-1
#5 Me You And Q.	4-1	7-5

In Quinn's opinion, the fans were overplaying the favorite while underplaying his top two choices. Correct strategy was for him to play both his top picks to win, which he did. (After deducting for the assured losing bet, the proper proportional betting amount for our $2000 capital chart would have been $20 on And Justice and $17 on Fond O'Green— though Quinn bet much more on each.) And Justice rolled to an easy wire-to-wire victory to return $10.80, and the day was off to a pleasant start.

1st Santa Anita

6 FURLONGS

(1.07¾) CLAIMING. Purse $18,000. 3-year olds and upward. Weights, 3-year olds, 120 lbs.; older, 122 lbs. Non-winners of two races since September 16 allowed 3 lbs.; of a race since then, 5 lbs.; since August 15, 7 lbs. Claiming price $20,000; if for $18,000, 2 lbs. (Races when entered for $16,000 or less not considered.)

*Fond O'Green

B. c. 4, by Irish River—Fondre, by Key to the Mint
Br.—Oak Cliff Thoroughbreds (Eng)
Tr.—Lewis Craig A

SOLIS A — 122
Own.—Moonshadow Stable

1987 9 3 1 0 $42,900
1986 1 M 0 0 $450
$20,000 Turf 1 0 0 0
Lifetime 10 3 1 0 $43,350

Kenai Dancer

B. g. 4, by Marshua's Dancer—Misty Clarion, by Proud Clarion
Br.—Harris W C (Ky)
Tr.—Stute Melvin F

VALENZUELA P A — 115
Own.—Edge Stable

1987 3 0 0 1 $1,080
1986 12 2 3 0 $14,765
$20,000
Lifetime 15 2 3 1 $15,845

Oh Dad

B. g. 6, by Tentam—Madam Irma, by Arts and Letters
Br.—Orenstein B & B (Md)
Tr.—Longden John E

GRYDER A T — 112⁵
Own.—Longden J E

1987 17 4 2 2 $48,162
1986 17 3 2 2 $23,935
$20,000 Turf 1 0 0 0 $675
Lifetime 53 10 4 11 $116,449

Dr. Reality

B. h. 7, by In Reality—Countess Fager, by Dr Fager
Br.—Robertson C J (Ky)
Tr.—Borick Robert

MEZA R Q — 113
Own.—Silver Light Stable
Entered 6Nov87- 9 SA

1987 4 0 0 0 $1,775
1986 12 2 2 2 $43,650
$18,000 Turf 5 0 0 0 $2,600
Lifetime 37 6 6 6 $147,895

Me You And Q. *

B. g. 4, by Search For Gold—Ara Star, by Pia Star
Br.—Arakelian Farms Inc (Cal)
Tr.—Threewitt Noble

PEDROZA M A — 115
Own.—Daniels Mrs T L

1987 19 3 5 4 $52,080
1986 18 4 3 2 $35,795
$20,000
Lifetime 42 7 8 6 $90,270

And Justice

B. g. 4, by Pledge Allegiance—Ethel Mermaid, by Crewman
Br.—Stoeven R (Cal)
Tr.—Luby Donn

STEVENS G L — 115
Own.—Elliott-Saidy-Stoeven

1986 3 1 0 0 $8,100
1985 1 M 0 0 $350
$20,000
Lifetime 4 1 0 0 $8,450

Since only six horses had been entered, Quinn didn't pay much attention to the place and show pools. He did check the daily double, which we'll review in a moment. He could have bet place and show in the first, though:

Total Pools	#1 Fond O'Green	#6 And Justice
Place $68,834	$6,867 (9.98%)	$9,018 (13.10%)
Show $38,951	$3,667 (9.41%)	$4,750 (12.19%)

According to our chart, we can bet a horse we make 3-1 in the place hole if he has 13.47% or less of that pool and to show if he has 11.99% or less; with 9.98% and 9.41%, Fond O'Green qualified for both. A horse we make 2-1 can be played with 17.97% and 15.99% to place and show, respectively; And Justice met both cutoff points. Had we bet the same amount on each horse, we would have profited—even though Fond O'Green failed, And Justice returned a healthy $6.00 to place and $5.00 to show, huge numbers in such a short field.

The second race was a maiden claiming event, the kind that Quinn normally refuses to even look at. Since I had given him the line-making assignment, however, he looked long enough to decide that only one horse even remotely interested him, a 12-1 morning-liner, #5, Cheyenne Tropic. He made the horse 5-2. Here were his daily double possibilities, along with the crowd's:

	Q	C
6-5 And Justice-Cheyenne Tropic	$31	$ 80
1-5 Fond O'Green-Cheyenne Tropic	$41	$143
5-5 Me You And Q.-Cheyenne Tropic	$52	$ 36

With his third choice an underlay, Quinn played the pair of big overlays (according to his line) in the double, 6-5 and 1-5. Cheyenne Tropic went off the second choice at 4-1, an overlay on Quinn's line. He also led from start to finish, and Quinn happily cashed not only the $10.20 win payoff but also a friendly $80.60 in the daily double.

A nice score—yet Quinn could have made even more on the race. First, check the complete run of daily double prices:

1-5	$143 (1.4%)
2-5	$ 76 (2.6%)
3-5	$ 82 (2.4%)
4-5	$129 (1.6%)
5-5	$ 36 (5.6%)
6-5	$ 80 (2.5%)

These percentages total only 16.1%, meaning Quinn could have assured himself odds of 5-1 on Cheyenne Tropic by betting him proportionally in the daily double (e.g., $14 on 1-5, $26 on 2-5, etc.) in addition to his overlay dd bet—and he still could have played the horse in the straight pool.

Second, Cheyenne Tropic could also have been bet to place and show. The maximum allowed percentages for a 5-2 shot are 15.40 and 13.71. These were Cheyenne Tropic's totals:

Place: $15,666 of $114,519 (13.68%)
Show: $ 9,174 of $ 73,975 (12.40%)

Cheyenne Tropic paid $10.20 to win, $6.20 to place, and $4.00 to show —generous prices considering that the 5-1 fourth choice was second and the 2-1 favorite finished third.

The third race looked like another three-horse race to Quinn. These were his contenders:

	Q	C
#5 Golden Gauntlet	5-2	3-5
#2 North Yard	4-1	7-2
#1 Cleverege	5-1	5-1

No value there, nor to place or show. Checking the $2 exacta payoffs, we found:

1-2 required $74, was paying $44
1-5 required $44, was paying $35
2-1 required $71, was paying $37
2-5 required $41, was paying $15
5-1 required $44, was paying $18
5-2 required $37, was paying $ 9

Nothing of interest. Quinn passed. Golden Gauntlet won at a measly $3.40, and the exacta with the longest shot in the six-horse field returned a dinky $29.20.

The fourth was a maiden claimer for 2-year-olds, for which Quinn refused to hazard any guess.

The fifth looked like an open contest:

	Q	C
#5 Pettrax	7-2	5-1
#6 Dennis D	9-2	5-2
#1 Bruli's Ante	5-1	5-2
#7 Passer II	5-1	5-1

3rd Santa Anita

6½ FURLONGS. (1.14) CLAIMING. Purse $23,000. 3-year-olds. Weight, 121 lbs. Non-winners of two races since September 1 allowed 3 lbs.; of a race since then, 5 lbs. Claiming price $50,000; if for $45,000, 2 lbs. (Races when entered for $40,000 or less not considered).

Cleverege

B. c. 3, by Clever Trick—Cherrywood Clover, by Porterhouse
PATTERSON A 116 Br.—Burburry G M & D D Jr (Ky) 1987 9 1 0 1 $17,060
Own.—Team Esprit Tr.—Garrison Rudy D $50,000 1986 6 1 3 0 $23,570
Lifetime 15 2 3 1 $40,630 Turf 1 0 0 0
Entered 6Nov87 8 SA
14Oct87-1SA 6f :214 :444 1:102ft 8½ 116 1hd 1½ 1hd 12½ Patterson A2 32000 86-16 Cleverg,HoustonBrgg,GrtNgotitor 11
3Oct87 8Fpx 6½f :213 :451 1:153ft 43 114 31½ 52¼ 69 614¾ Patterson A4 Aw28000 83-10 Little Red Cloud,MiBeso,TokyoBoy 7
20Sep87-10Fpx 6½f :211 :453 1:172ft 19 115 31 96¾ 911 714 Patterson A1 Aw25000 75-16 JustNeverMind,Krestig,Ack'sRply 10
9Sep87-7Dmr 1 1/16 ⓣ:48 1:1231:441fm 18 117 64 74¾ 107¼ 108½ Patterson A1 Aw24000 70-21 WishfulThinkr,JohnVgors,BrdDncr 10
2Sep87-3Dmr 6½f :213 :442 1:161ft 14 114 32½ 31½ 42 35¼ Patterson A7 50000 86-17 Silver Hero,SilentImpact,Cleverege 7
22Aug87-5Dmr 6½f :22 :451 1:154ft 74 114 104 105¾ 107 511½ Patterson A7 Aw22000 82-15 Light Sabre, Danski, RaiseAPound 12
8Aug87-10LA 6f :211 :442 1:101ft 35 113 68½ 69 818 810 PttersonA8 ⓡDn Bnlo 82-13 StepSon,Extranix,He'sADncingMn 10
24Jan87-3SA 6f :212 :442 1:101ft 10 118 32¾ 32½ 45½ 69¼ Patterson A5 Aw26000 78-18 HppyInSpc,SwtwtrSprings,ThQuppr 9
10Jan87-3SA 6½f :223 :454 1:172gd 6 119 31½ 32¾ 33½ 44¼ Patterson A2 Aw26000 79-20 PrinceSssfrs,ThQuippr,WstrlyWind 6
27Dec86-7SA 6f :214 :451 1:104ft 14e 120 2hd 1hd 1hd 2nk Patterson A5 Aw26000 84-19 SocilDimond,Cleverege,WstrlyWind 8
27Dec86—Bumped intervals late
Oct 22 SA 4f ft :492 h Sep 28 SA tr.t 3f ft :372 h ●Sep 19 SA tr.t 3f ft :361 h

North Yard

B. g. 3, by Messenger of Song—Maui, by Hawaii
STEVENS G L 118 Br.—Carver Stable (Cal) 1987 8 2 3 2 $34,190
Own.—Summa Stable Tr.—Feld Jude T $50,000 1986 3 1 1 1 $4,135
Lifetime 11 3 4 3 $38,325
25Oct87-6SA 6½f :214 :45 1:172gd *8-5 118 3½ 3½ 4¾ 32¼ Stevens G L5 c40000 81-19 Cooper,WeWannaWinner,NorthYrd 7
25Oct87—Wide in stretch
11Oct87-10TuP 6f :212 :441 1:093ft 2¾ 117 1hd 1hd 1hd 2½ PttrsA5 Hwkns Spcl H 85-18 SonyBlum,NorthYard,NturllyLucky 6
21Sep87-10Fpx 6½f :213 :452 1:171ft 7 115 11½ 11 11½ 11¼ Hansen R D10 Aw25000 90-15 NorthYrd,LittleRedCloud,DryRidg 10
29Aug87-2Dmr 6f :213 :442 1:092ft 6 116 1½ 1hd 1hd 31¾ Meza R Q4 40000 89-12 GoldnGntlt,SwtwtrSprngs,NrthYrd 10
6Aug87-1Dmr 6f :212 :441 1:09 ft 19 118 21 22½ 23½ 28 Meza R Q4 40000 85-15 Robert'sLd,NorthYrd,HedlineNws 10
12Jun87-8Cby 6½f :223 :454 1:182ft *4-5 112 51¼ 41 2hd 16 LaGrange D L6 Aw9500 89-18 NorthYrd,BiscyneBoy,Brend'sFrind 8
28May87-9Cby 6f :222 :454 1:112ft 2 114 31½ 31 2hd 2½ LaGrange D L4 Aw9500 88-19 SavorFire,NorthYrd,VictoriousStud 8
14May87-9Cby 6f :222 :454 1:113ft 13 112 32 33 42 32 LaGrangeDL6 Aw11500 86-16 Tavi'sWizrd,TurnBckJohn,NorthYrd 9
14May87—Disqualified from purse money
28Nov86-9TuP 6f :22 :444 1:092ft 3½ 120 1½ 1½ 1½ 21¼ SteinbergPW3 Aw5200 87-15 SonyBlum,NorthYard,Justlittleloot 8
15Nov86-2TuP 6f :214 :452 1:102ft 5 118 2hd 11 11½ 1hd Wentz M8 Mdn 84-16 NorthYrd,ArrestMeRd,MndmiWys 11
Oct 6 SA 4f ft :492 h Sep 30 SA 5f ft 1:014 h Sep 17 SA 3f ft :362 h Sep 12 Dmr 4f ft :492 h

Rising Pine

B. g. 3, by Rising Market—Pining, by Olympiad King
PATTON D R 118 Br.—Russell C (Cal) 1987 3 1 0 0 $11,970
Own.—ConnorJr-Moorr-RsngPnSyn Tr.—Christensen Reid $50,000 1986 0 M 0 0
Lifetime 3 1 0 0 $11,970
16Oct87-7SA 6f :22 :451 1:092ft 45 1135 11 42¾ 79½ 720 Gryder A T8 50000 71-17 GrndVizier,GoldenGuntlt,NkdJybird 8
16Oct87—Fanned wide throughout by loose horse
3Oct87-7Fpx 6½f :213 :452 1:183ft 19 114 43 31½ 11½ 11 Sorenson D2 Mdn 83-10 RisingPine,BonzoWilli,MotorCityLd 9
3Oct87—Bumped start
26Sep87-6Fpx 6½f :22 :453 1:173ft 8½ 114 98½ 59 610 615¾ Patterson A2 Mdn 72-11 SensationalStr,Gslighter,Vysotsky 10
Nov 4 SA 5f sl 1:013 h Oct 28 SA 1 ft 1:422 h Sep 17 Fpx 7f ft 1:293 h Sep 12 Fpx 4f ft :474 hg

Diarmaid

Dk. b. or br. c. 3, by Ack Ack—Ganttown Legend, by Get Around
CASTANON A L 116 Br.—Franks J (La) 1986 1 M 0 1 $2,700
Own.—Crowley & Downey Tr.—Jordan James $50,000
Lifetime 1 0 0 1 $2,700
29Nov86-5Hol 6f :22 :453 1:103ft 12 118 31 31½ 32 31¾ Pincay L Jr 2 Mdn 88-12 OrchardSong,SocilDimond,Dirmid 10
29Nov86—Bumped break
Nov 4 SA 4f sl :511 h Oct 30 SA 5f gd 1:01 h Oct 25 SA 5f gd 1:021 h Oct 21 SA 5f ft 1:062 h

Golden Gauntlet

Ch. c. 3, by Golden Eagle II—Air of Elegance, by Dr Fager
MCCARRON C J 116 Br.—Mabee Mr-Mrs J C (Cal) 1987 7 2 1 0 $26,600
Own.—Golden Eagle Farm Tr.—Sadler John W $50,000 1986 1 1 0 0 $6,600
Lifetime 8 3 1 0 $33,200
16Oct87-7SA 6f :22 :451 1:092ft 2¾ 117 41½ 22½ 21½ 21¾ Pincay L Jr 7 50000 89-17 GrndVizier,GoldenGuntlt,NkdJybird 8
8Oct87-5SA 6½f :214 :443 1:154ft 4½ 117 42½ 33 43½ 43¼ Pincay L Jr 2 ⓢAw28000 88-19 MiBeso,TimeForSkrto,Brid'sAdvic 12
13Sep87-3Dmr 1 1/16 :46 1:112 1:434ft 3½ 117 22 2hd 2½ 46½ Pincay L Jr 2 Aw24000 74-18 ChessSet,CircleViewDrive,Mondnit 6
13Sep87—Lugged out
29Aug87-2Dmr 6f :213 :442 1:092ft 3¾ 116 64½ 43½ 32 1½ McCarron C J 10 40000 91-12 GoldnGntlt,SwtwtrSprngs,NrthYrd 10
29Aug87—Poor start
14Aug87-3Dmr 6½f :22 :451 1:163ft 8½ 113 63½ 68½ 54½ 55 Pincay L Jr 1 ⓢAw21000 84-17 IrishRobbery,FancyOats,TahoeTngo 6
14Aug87—Veered in, stumbled start; lugged out 3/8
1Mar87-3SA 6½f :221 :45 1:162ft 3½ 114 1hd 1hd 3½ 42¾ Black C A 8 ⓢAw27000 84-15 HollywoodSrnd,Rconnoitring,OBtth 6
16Feb87-3SA 6f :213 :443 1:104gd 4½ 118 56 44½ 33½ 12¼ ‡Black C A 4 32000 84-21 OkWine,GoldenGuntlet,ShrewdStev 7
16Feb87—Broke in a tangle, bumped; checked at 3/16; ‡Dead heat
24Dec86-6Hol 6f :22 :453 1:112ft 12 118 31½ 21 21 1no Black C A 5 ⓢM32000 86-20 GoldenGauntlet,OBtth,VikingBlue 12
Nov 4 SA 4f sl :473 h Oct 27 SA 4f ft :471 h Oct 6 SA 3f ft :374 h ●Sep 30 SA 6f ft 1:12 h

Gold Room

B. g. 3, by Racing Room—Galdore, by Twist the Axe
GRYDER A T 1095 Br.—Sheehy Dr P F (Ky) 1987 13 1 5 2 $33,270
Own.—Johnson W R Tr.—Arena Joseph $45,000 1986 1 M 0 0 $300
Lifetime 14 1 5 2 $33,570
22Oct87-9SA 1 1/16 :471 1:131 1:472sy 9 1115 912 66 31 22¼ Gryder A T2 32000 62-35 Boo W., Gold Room, Compound 12
22Oct87—Very wide into stretch
12Oct87-9SA 1 1/16 :48 1:121 1:433ft 3½ 116 66½ 811 69½ 59¾ McCarron C J6 40000 73-15 ElTremblor,‡DineAtTen,P T.Hustler 8
12Oct87—Broke slowly
19Sep87-10Fpx 1 1/16 :48 1:133 1:451ft 3½ 114 73½ 85¾ 77¾ 78½ Pedroza MA7 Aw27000 76-18 Bugarian, Proving Spark, Shrewdy 10
10Sep87-3Dmr 1 1/16 :46 1:103 1:422ft 3 116 56½ 53 53 23½ McCarron C J2 c40000 84-14 Talk'sCheap,GoldRoom,ElTremblor 6
26Aug87-9Dmr 1 1/16 :46 1:111 1:432ft 4 116 811 65½ 32½ 2½ Baze R A8 32000 82-15 Someshine, Gold Room,P T Hustler 9
26Aug87—Wide 3/8 turn; lugged in stretch
14Aug87 9Dmr 1 1/16 :454 1:103 1:44 ft 14 116 76½ 55½ 33½ 42¾ Baze R A1 40000 77-17 GrndVizier,GryAloh,You'rGlorious 10
14Aug87—Bumped hard start
30May87-2Hol 1 :46 1:113 1:382ft 3¾ 115 44½ 42½ 21 1nk Stevens G L9 M40000 71-14 Gold Room,CrystalFox,SuperJimmy 9
7May87-6Hol 1 :444 1:10 1:37 ft 4 115 87¾ 74¼ 43½ 31½ Stevens G L6 M50000 77-13 Terror Eyes,CrystalFox,GoldRoom 12
22Apr87-6Hol 1 1/16 :46 1:114 1:441ft 3½ 115 88¼ 43 33½ 31¾ Stevens G L5 M50000 86-18 Brber'sChoice,SirTyson,GoldRoom 10
11Apr87-4SA 1 :462 1:113 1:374ft *2½ 117 44 52½ 41½ 24½ Ortega L E 2 M50000 74-16 FvDddyFv,GoldRoom,LttlArgumnt 10
Oct 9 SA 5f ft 1:002 h Oct 2 SA 5f ft :592 h

5th Santa Anita

1 1-16 MILES
SANTA ANITA

1 1/16 MILES. (1.40½) CLAIMING. Purse $22,000. 3-year-olds and upward. Weights, 3-year-olds, 118 lbs.; older, 121 lbs. Non-winners of two races at one mile or over since September 1 allowed 3 lbs.; of such a race since then, 5 lbs. Claiming price $25,000; if for $22,500 allowed 2 lbs. (Claiming and starter races for $20,000 or less not considered.)

Bruli's Ante ✶

Ch. g. 4, by Raise a Bid—Bruli Kaan, by Bold and Brave
Br.—Game Racing Farm (Tex)
Own.—Slutzky&WinningWaysStable
STEVENS G L 116 Tr.—Stein Roger

| | 1987 | 22 | 3 | 6 | 6 | $62,015 |
| 1986 | 16 | 3 | 6 | 5 | $33,685 |

Lifetime 20 6 11 $95,700

Morry's Champ

Gr. h. 7, by Don B—Kamadora, by Fleet Nasl
Br.—King Brothers Stable (Cal)
Own.—Alpert & Fanning
HAWLEY S 116 Tr.—Fanning Jerry

1987	11	1	0	1	$17,525
1986	7	0	1	1	$13,500
Turf	46	4	4	5	$142,162

Lifetime 71 6 8 8 $204,212

Flying Gene

Ch. g. 8, by Real Value—Spanish Riches, by Pieces of Eight II
Br.—Wedgewood Farm (Ky)
Own.—Fowler-MacDonald-Wytt
VERGARA O 114 Tr.—MacDonald Norman S

1987	10	0	0	2	$8,750
1986	9	0	1	0	$14,375
Turf	57	3	4	6	$150,900

Lifetime 86 4 9 19 $263,450

Bold Decree

B. c. 4, by Bold L B—Sweet Kakki Briar, by Etonian
Br.—Jones B C (Ky)
Own.—Pendleton L C
GRYDER A T 1115 Tr.—Lewis Craig A

1987	8	0	0	1	$4,575
1986	7	2	0	3	$34,125
Turf	2	0	0	0	

Lifetime 18 3 2 5 $52,400

Pettrax ✕

B. g. 5, by Petrone—Roman Dame, by British Roman
Br.—Charlton B (Cal)
Own.—Charlton B W
BLACK C A 114 Tr.—Charlton Wayne

1987	11	1	2	1	$30,750
1986	12	4	2	1	$91,700
Turf	36	6	5	2	$209,325

Lifetime 76 16 14 5 $527,836

Dennis D.

Gr. g. 4, by Hawkin's Special—Wink an Eye, by Stop the Music
Br.—Malmuth Mr-Mrs M (Ky)
Own.—Friedman & Stephen
McCARRON C J 118 Tr.—Mitchell Mike

| 1987 | 8 | 2 | 1 | 1 | $29,855 |
| 1986 | 9 | 1 | 1 | 2 | $12,650 |

Lifetime 18 3 2 3 $42,400

*Passer II ✶

Dk. b. or br. c. 4, by Irish Conn—Curious Carolyn, by Wig Out
Br.—Navarro J S (Mex)
Own.—Buck-Cain-Rianda
BANDERAS A L 1115 Tr.—State Melvin F

1987	15	1	0	1	$22,862
1986	11	0	2	1	$37,325
Turf	3	0	0	0	$143,864

Lifetime 29 3 3 2 $143,864

The exactas didn't offer much. Quinn bet the minor overlay, Pettrax. The horse was in contention till the stretch, then tired. The winner was Dennis D, the slight favorite over Bruli's Ante. The 6-1 exacta returned just $52 for $5; Quinn's required number was $200. Even if he had made both horses 5-2 on his line, $52 was too short.

The sixth race was the start of the pick 3, known as the daily triple at Santa Anita. The opener was another maiden filly claimer, so Quinn switched on the no-betting sign. He did discuss the race with me, though, so I could play the pick 3.

He liked the favorite, Designing Charles, though her even-money price was no thrill. She had turned in a powerful race against straight maiden fillies last time out. He also gave some chance to Smart Deception, the mystery horse; in her debut seven weeks earlier, she had survived a horribly troubled trip to finish fourth, and was picking up top jockey Chris McCarron. He hated second choice Hug A Lot, who had managed to stop in the stretch in every lifetime start.

Quinn also told me he disliked the entire seventh race intensely, and loved Ferdinand in the eighth-race feature. I then made up this pick 3 chart, with my own guesstimates of each horse's win chances:

6th—	5 Designing Charles	.50
	4 Smart Deception	.20
7th—	4 Dawn Of Hope	.30
	3 Jell	.25
	5 Miss Beverly Hills	.20
8th—	6 Ferdinand	.60

I then multiplied the win chances of each three-horse series, and bet accordingly:

5-4-6	9.0%	$18
5-3-6	7.5%	$15
5-5-6	6.0%	$12
4-4-6	3.6%	$ 7
4-3-6	3.0%	$ 6
4-5-6	2.4%	$ 5

It was time to turn back to the tote board for the sixth race. Designing Charles was an overlay to show, with barely 20% of the pool. I bet her to show. At the wire, she was nailed by Smart Deception, who returned $16.60. Designing Charles finished second and I collected $2.60 to show.

The seventh race was another no-bet for Quinn, since every horse he had liked in the morning was scratched. My pick 3 was swatted away

6th Santa Anita

6 FURLONGS
SANTA ANITA

6 FURLONGS. (1.07⅘) MAIDEN CLAIMING. Purse $17,000. Fillies. 2-year-olds. Weight, 117 lbs. Claiming price $50,000; if for $45,000 allowed 2 lbs.

Coupled—Hug A Lot and Summer Alliance.

```
Solar Empress                    B. f. 2, by Tudor Blue—Queen's Salute, by Solar Salute
                                 Br.—Boyce O (Cal)                          1987 3 M 0 0      $300
  MIRANDA V              1125    Tr.—Layne Arthur F             $50,000
Own.—Layne A F                   Lifetime  3 0 0 0   $300
11Oct87-6Fno   6f :223 :464 1:123ft   11 1125  53½ 31½ 53 45½   Miranda V5   ⒻMdn 71-18 InksBlst,ForVerblim,S'CoopOfVnill 8
10Oct87-8Fpx   6f :221 :462 1:132ft   62 116   1014 914 916 918½ Winick D9   ⒻⓈMdn 62-14 SlutThGls,StdySistr,ColorfulFlight 10
7Sep87-3Dmr    6½f :223 :453 1:17 ft  42 117   79 813 820 829½  Winick D1    ⒻⓈMdn 57-14 Petchik,PresentFlyer,PetiteFemme 8
     7Sep87—Ducked out start; raced greenly

Veronica's Macumba               B. f. 2, by Messenger of Song—Conestoga Flash, by Conestoga
                                 Br.—Pacifica Thoroughbreds (Cal)          1987 1 M 0 0
  BLACK C A              117     Tr.—Needham Lloyd              $50,000
Own.—B Lucky Stable              Lifetime  1 0 0 0
29Oct87 2SA    6f :22 :453 1:113gd    59 117                    Olivares F10 ⒻM40000      Invierno, Marivett, Hug A Lot  12
     29Oct87—Pulled up
  Nov 4 SA 4f sl :49 hg     Oct 26 GD tr.t 4f ft :49 h     Oct 19 GD tr.t 5f ft 1:013 h     Oct 6 GD tr.t 5f ft 1:014 h

Sadie B. Fast                    Ch. f. 2, by Fast—Jaded Sadie, by Don B
                                 Br.—Pascoe W T III (Cal)                   1987 0 M 0 0
  PEDROZA M A            115     Tr.—Moerman Gerald C           $45,000
Own.—Foster W J                  Lifetime  0 0 0 0
  Nov 2 SA 3f m :37 h       Oct 26 SA 4f ft :501 h     Oct 21 SA 5f ft 1:024 h     Oct 16 SA 4f ft :494 h

Smart Deception                  Ch. f. 2, by Red Ryder—La Deception, by Smarten
                                 Br.—Cahan M (Ky)                           1987 1 M 0 0      $1,400
  MCCARRON C J           117     Tr.—Spawr William              $50,000
Own.—Sell C                      Lifetime  1 0 0 0   $1,400
17Sep87-4Fpx   6½f :221 :462 1:173ft   5 116   911 914 912 414½ Hansen R D7  ⒻMdn 73-12 PrncssRy,LovYoDrlng,Bshp'sRqst 10
     17Sep87—Hopped in air, broke out, bumped
  Nov 4 SA 4f sl :504 h     Oct 27 SA 5f ft 1:023 h     Oct 22 SA 4f ft :502 h     Oct 7 SA 5f ft :593 h

Designing Charles                B. f. 2, by In Tissar—Jerell's Girl, by Raise Your Glass
                                 Br.—Halo Farms (Cal)                       1987 2 M 2 0      $7,000
  HAWLEY S               117     Tr.—Rose Larry                 $50,000
Own.—Halo Farms                  Lifetime  2 0 2 0   $7,000
24Oct87-3SA    6f :214 :444 1:103gd   6½ 117   32½ 33½ 33 23    Pincay L Jr4 ⒻMdn 82-17 LtsFllInLov,DsigningChrls,ComclCt 7
9Oct87-4SA     6f :213 :46 1:13 ft    17 1125  34 42½ 43½ 2½    Magallon P1  ⒻM32000 72-17 LHonyGrl,DsgnngChrls,BtflBgnng 11
  Oct 21 SA 5f ft 1:013 h   Oct 7 SA 3f ft :351 h     Oct 1 SA 6f ft 1:144 hg     Sep 25 SA 6f ft 1:151 hg

Hello Cutie                      B. f. 2, by Dimaggio—Hello High, by El Gran Capitan
                                 Br.—Valpredo J & D (Cal)                   1987 6 M 1 0      $5,900
  GRYDER A T             1105    Tr.—Guiney Irv                 $45,000
Own.—Valpredo J                  Lifetime  6 0 1 0   $5,900
29Oct87-6SA    6f :22 :454 1:121gd     6 117   105¾109½119¾109  Solis A9     ⒻM40000 68-16 SuperAvie,Chipadedod,FlutterBug 12
     29Oct87—Stumbled start; took up 5 1/2
8Oct87-6SA     6f :221 :462 1:113ft   20 1125  33½ 32 62¾ 57½   Patton D B10 ⒻⓈMdn 72-19 VrietyBby,TbleForNshu,SpedOnTp 11
23Sep87-8Fpx   1⅛:46 1:122 1:461ft    27 1115  32 2hd 1hd 2¾    Banderas A L4 ⒻMdn 79-12 JansJn,HelloCutie,FounderOfThrills 9
     23Sep87—Steadied early
11Sep87-6Dmr   6f :22 :451 1:104ft    37 115   1111 98¾ 99½ 811¼ Ortega L E2 ⒻM45000 73-13 AffordblPrc,LpOfLuxury,T V Tussl 12
     11Sep87—Green down backstretch
27Aug87-6Dmr   6f :222 :46 1:114ft    8½ 115   42 43½ 44½ 48½   Sibille R3   ⒻM45000 71-17 May First, ComeRussian,HugALot 12
23Jly87-4Hol   6f :224 :471 1:132ft   15 117   86 87½ 57 45½    CstnonAL9 ⒻⓈM40000 70-15 Tis Fast, It's Silver, Fleet Saros 12
     23Jly87—Poor start
  Nov 5 SA 3f sy :364 h (d)  Oct 29 SA 3f ft :361 h   Oct 22 SA 6f ft 1:143 h     Oct 15 SA 5f ft 1:023 h

Perone                           Dk. b. or br. f. 2, by Perrault—One More Bid, by Personality
                                 Br.—Martin Mr-Mrs C A (Ky)                 1987 0 M 0 0
  OLIVARES F             115     Tr.—Fanning Jerry              $45,000
Own.—Martin Mr-Mrs C A           Lifetime  0 0 0 0
  Oct 30 SA 5f gd 1:013 hg  Oct 24 SA 4f sy :504 h    Oct 18 SA 5f ft 1:004 h     Oct 12 SA 5f ft 1:001 h

Kelly's Lass                     B. f. 2, by Sham—Kelly's Thief, by No Robbery
                                 Br.—Looney J (Cal)                         1987 4 M 0 0      $1,040
  BAZE G                 117     Tr.—Niccoli Roger              $50,000
Own.—Stephens G                  Lifetime  4 0 0 0   $1,040
3Oct87-4Fpx    6f :223 :462 1:121ft   42 115   67 67½ 58 49     PttersonA10  ⓈM32000 77-10 VegsKey,Hgly'sLion,PubliclyPropr 10
17Sep87-4Fpx   6½f :221 :462 1:173ft  47 116   54½ 56 710 818½  Higuera A R9 ⒻMdn 70-12 PrncssRy,LovYoDrlng,Bshp'sRqst 10
23Jly87-4Hol   6f :224 :471 1:132ft   17 115   97½1112111310 14½ Mena F3    ⒻⓈM35000 61-15 Tis Fast, It's Silver, Fleet Saros 12
     23Jly87  Hopped in air
10Jly87-4Hol   5½f :223 :462 1:042ft   5½ 117  87¾109¾ 913 822¾ McCrrCJ9   ⒻⓈM40000 69-14 It'sAnothrTrn,HrdToFthm,MrysGl 10
     10Jly87—Bumped, bobbled start; bore out 3/8 turn
  Oct 28 Fpx 4f ft :501 h   Oct 14 SA 5f ft 1:022 h   Sep 27 SA 3f ft :354 h      Sep 14 SA 5f ft 1:022 h

Telletiquette                    B. f. 2, by Tell—Snootie Poly, by Vested Power
                                 Br.—Berliner N & Toni (Cal)                1987 1 M 0 0
  VERGARA O              115     Tr.—Davis Mark                 $45,000
Own.—Smith D R                   Lifetime  1 0 0 0
15Jly87-6Hol   6f :214 :453 1:104ft  146 117   64½1112111311 23½ Patterson A5 ⒻMdn 66-14 Sheeshm,PrtyInProgrss,PrsntFlyr 11
  Oct 17 Fpx 5f ft 1:032 h  ●Sep 30 Fpx 4f ft :47 hg  Sep 19 Fpx 3f ft :374 h

Golden Mint Mark                 Ch. f. 2, by Plugged Nickle—Decide, by Bold Reason
                                 Br.—Heritage Thorbrd Associates (Ky)       1987 0 M 0 0
  VALENZUELA P A         117     Tr.—Manzi Joseph               $50,000
Own.—Jackson & Koppe             Lifetime  0 0 0 0
  Nov 4 SA 5f sl 1:031 h    Oct 19 SA 4f ft :491 hg   Oct 10 SA 4f ft :48 h       Oct 5 SA 6f ft 1:152 h

Hug A Lot                        B. f. 2, by Raise a Cup—Hugable, by Warfare
                                 Br.—Calumet Farm (Ky)                      1987 6 M 0 2      $4,825
  STEVENS G L            115     Tr.—Lukas D Wayne              $45,000
Own.—Calumet Farm Inc            Lifetime  6 0 0 2   $4,825
29Oct87-2SA    6f :22 :453 1:113gd   *2½ 117   21½ 33½ 32½ 34½  Pincay L Jr1 ⒻM40000 75-16 Invierno, Marivett, Hug A Lot 12
     29Oct87—Drifted out
18Oct87-4SA    6f :221 :453 1:094ft   9½ 117   32 44½ 410 618½  Pincay L Jr3 ⒻMdn 70-15 JennJons,Forwrning,Smrtrthnilook 8
27Aug87-6Dmr   6f :222 :46 1:114ft    11 117   3½ 31½ 33½ 34¾   McCrronCJ6   ⒻM50000 74-17 May First, ComeRussian,HugALot 12
13Aug87-6Dmr   6f :221 :462 1:12 ft   14 117   62¾ 74¾ 87¼ 914  VlenzuelPA9  ⒻM50000 64-20 Valid Allure, Petchik, Allocate 12
     13Aug87—Bumped 1/2, 3/8
22Jly87-4Hol   6f :22 :453 1:114ft    11 117   44 78½ 710 715   Stevens G L5 ⒻMdn 69-15 Bolchina, Teach Me, Pirate's Angel 7
19Jun87-4Hol   5½f :221 :46 1:051ft   2¾ 117   1hd 2hd 34½ 510½ Stevens G L3 ⒻMdn 77-14 Acurare, Crown Catcher, Slide Jet 7
  Oct 10 SA 4f ft :471 hg   Oct 5 SA 4f ft :493 h     Sep 27 SA 5f ft 1:022 h     Sep 16 Dmr 4f ft :474 h
```

9th Santa Anita

1 MILE

SANTA ANITA

1 MILE. (1.33⅗) CLAIMING. Purse $13,000. 3-year-olds and upward. Weights, 3-year-olds, 118 lbs.; older, 121 lbs. Non-winners of two races at 1 mile or over since September 1 allowed 3 lbs.; of such a race since then 5 lbs. Claiming price $10,000. (Races when entered for $8,500 or less not considered.)

Reason To Study

B. g. 4, by Coulee Man—Mag's Deck, by Mo Bay
STEVENS G L 116 Br.—Smith & Quisenberry (Cal) 1987 4 0 2 0 $4,700
Own.—Academic Farms Inc Tr.—Truman Eddie $10,000 1986 9 2 1 0 $19,050
Lifetime 14 2 3 0 $24,575
12Sep87-2Dmr 1 :462 1:103 1:363ft 3½ 116 41½ 22½ 25 35½ McCarron C J 3 10000 79-14 InToto,‡BoldSaintPt,ResonToStudy 8
12Sep87—Bumped start; bumped hard 1/8, 1/16; Placed second through disqualification
24Aug87-9Dmr 1⅛ :453 1:104 1:492ft 14 116 56 86¼ 1116 1020 Kaenel J L 2 12500 63-17 L.A.Fire,WonderPlum,BronzTudor 12
24Aug87—Bumped start
31Jly87-1Dmr 1 1/16 :471 1:123 1:451ft *6-5 116 1½ 1½ 2½ 2½ Stevens G L 2 10000 73-17 Parlpino,ResonToStudy,Preservtive 9
19Jly87-1Hol 1 1/16 :461 1:111 1:434ft 3 115 2hd 32½ 46½ 59½ Stevens G L 1 10000 80-07 ExotcArbtor,JollyJosh,S'LongFrwll 9
13Nov86-7Hol 1⅛ :472 1:122 1:521ft 6 116 41¼ 64½ 88 97¼ Kaenel J L 8 20000 69-23 HertbrkDncr,JupitrTog,DoublQust 10
16Oct86-9SA 1 1/16 :472 1:122 1:44 ft 9 118 21 2½ 24 26¼ Kaenel J L 2 20000 74-19 CojakMan,ResonToStudy,Averted 10
9Oct86-9SA 1 1/16 :472 1:122 1:451ft 12 115 65 84½ 85¾ 77¾ Kaenel J L 5 22500 67-21 ILoveRcing,MimiDrem,HrtbrkDncr 12
9Oct86—Bumped; wide
28Aug86-7Dmr 1 1/16 :45 1:104 1:442ft 8¾ 116 69½ 58 68¾ 48¾ Kaenel J L 11 25000 69-18 Averted,ILoveRacing,MiamiDream 11
14Aug86-9Dmr 1 1/16 :462 1:113 1:443ft 8¼ 116 31½ 21 22 1½ Kaenel J L 5 20000 77-17 ReasonToStudy,MimiDrem,Averted 9
31Jly86-9Dmr 1 1/16 :46 1:11 1:433ft 9 116 1hd 31½ 44½ 58½ Kaenel J L 2 25000 73-12 LewrdPirt,BlowThTrumpts,RidgFlit 9
31Jly86—Broke in a tangle
●Oct 24 SA tr.t 6f gd 1:142 h Oct 16 SA 5f ft 1:011 h Oct 9 SA 5f ft 1:004 h Sep 30 SA 4f ft :49 h

Fabulous Gaelic

B. c. 4, by Somethingfabulous—Bencina, by Gaelic Dancer
SOLIS A 116 Br.—Fellows A (Cal) 1987 11 2 2 1 $11,485
Own.—Borrell A J Tr.—Miyadi Steve $10,000 1986 4 M 0 1 $1,400
Lifetime 16 2 2 2 $12,885
1Nov87-1SA 6f :212 :443 1:101m 3½ 116 714 712 69½ 54½ DelahoussayeE 5 12500 82-12 CoursingEagle,Witching,JulioNMe 7
22Oct87-1SA 6f :221 :454 1:121ft 17 116 1110 86½ 35 31½ Solis A 6 [S] 10000 75-25 AirPirte,Polly'sRuler,FbulousGelc 12
27Jly87-1Hol 1 :454 1:111 1:374ft 9 115 65 54 64½ 63¼ Solis A 4 10000 71-11 Hrdtohndle,RopTndr,ExoticArbitor 8
11Jly87-2Hol 1 :451 1:101 1:362ft 6¾ 118 79½ 89½ 89 99 Stevens G L 9 10000 72-12 Ayaabi,SrosChick,ElectricMoment 11
1Jly87-2Hol 7f :222 :451 1:242ft 92 115 1011 98½ 54 1no Solis A 10 10000 82-13 FblosGlc,ElctrcMmnt,DmndCttrII 11
24May87-9Hol 1⅛ :472 1:12 1:511ft 29 116 42½ 56 712 916½ McHargue D G 8 10000 64-13 Nostradmus,ExoticArbitor,Disciple 9
4Apr87-9AC 1 :51 1:144 1:402hy 13 115 2hd 2hd 2hd 2nk Delgadillo C 5 10000 71-29 ProprMrk,FbulousGlc,BoldNntquos 6
4Apr87—Broke poorly
15Mar87-11AC 1 1/16 :482 1:123 1:47 m 9-5 120 67½ 49 11½ 11½ Delgadillo C 3 M4000 70-23 FabulousGaelic,Outsider,BillPayer 11
1Mar87-11AC 6f :23 :452 1:101ft 3½ 120 63 54 43 44¼ Delgadillo C 4 M6250 84-16 Herald'sTerne,Steadfastness,Rozmr 9
1Feb87-2AC 6f :221 :443 1:10 ft 6½ 118 86¼ 79 65¾ 25 Lopez A D 2 M5750 84-15 Wody'sWnnr,FblsGlc,DplmtcLgnd 12
Oct 16 SA 6f ft 1:144 h Oct 10 SA 5f ft 1:011 h Oct 3 SA 5f ft 1:02 h Sep 28 SA 5f ft 1:021 h

Majestuso

B. g. 5, by L'Heureux—Crepe de Glace, by West Coast Scout
PEDROZA M A 116 Br.—Downing C G (Ky) 1987 21 5 5 5 $20,646
Own.—Chase D F Tr.—Sinne Gerald M $10,000 1985 13 0 2 4 $18,325
Lifetime 36 6 7 10 $41,110
29Oct87-9SA 1 1/16 :462 1:111 1:44 gd 6¾ 116 41¼ 31¼ 32 34 Pedroza M A 3 10000 77-16 Equilibre, Nostradamus, Majestuso 11
24Oct87-1SA 6f :212 :45 1:103gd 9 116 78¾ 67¾ 55½ 56 Pedroza M A 7 10000 79-17 Cool'nScndlos,Lrl'sTm,HvrngPrsnc 9
24Oct87—Broke slowly
16Oct87-1SA 6f :22 :45 1:104ft 8¼ 116 1112 1114 1011 911¼ Kaenel J L 1 10000 73-17 Doodlesack, Witching, Tigerillo 12
16Oct87—Fanned wide into stretch
2Oct87-9Fpx 1 1/16 :463 1:121 1:45 ft 4¾ 114 1hd 11 1hd 21½ Sorenson D 4 10500 85-13 OlimpicBingo,Mjstuso,ForvrBluJns 9
24Sep87-13Fpx a1⅛ :463 1:121 1:503ft 8½ 114 2hd 3nk 37 310½ Sorenson D 3 A8500 79-16 Siraluovat, Jolly Josh, Majestuso 6
24Sep87—Bobbled 1st turn
15Aug87-9AC 1 :453 1:093 1:343ft 2½ 114 11½ 12 1hd 2½ Enriquez H F 5 10000 99-13 BoldInititive,Mjestuso,CuttingLine 6
4Aug87-5AC 1 :461 1:10 1:352ft *2¼ 114 41 3½ 3nk 32¾ Enriquez H F 4 Aw6000 93-12 Trouble T., Forio, Majestuso 5
25Jly87-9AC 1 :463 1:103 1:364ft *2-3 115 11½ 13 2hd 33 Enriquez H F 8 10000 86-19 Bold Initiative,TroubleT.,Majestuso 8
11Jly87-9AC 1 1/16 :463 1:102 1:412ft 5½ 114 22 2hd 21 24 HernndezMG 3 Aw6000 94-13 PolAndDic,Majestuso,ActiveRomar 9
20Jun87-10AC 1 :453 1:093 1:352ft *8-5 114 11½ 13 11½ 1hd Enriquez H F 5 8000 96-12 Mjestuso,PolAndDic,PocketRocket 8
Sep 18 Fpx 7f ft 1:273 h

Rope Tender

B. g. 5, by Royal Derby II—Penny Betty, by Catchpenny II
BANDERAS A L 1115 Br.—McKee D (Cal) 1987 12 3 2 0 $13,958
Own.—Floyd & San Miguel Tr.—Salazar Mario $10,000 1986 5 1 2 1 $8,461
Lifetime 34 4 7 3 $33,519
18Oct87-9Fno 1 :453 1:11 1:37 ft *8-5 116 76½ 75½ 2½ 11½ Noguez A M 3 5000 84-13 RopeTendr,ThLstDrgon,TotlRqust 10
11Oct87-13Fno 1 :47 1:13 1:38 ft 2¾ 121 75½ 52¾ 32 12½ Noguez A M 6 3500 79-18 Rope Tender, Flying Lime, Eterno 9
4Oct87-5Fpx 1 1/16 :473 1:13 1:45 ft 6 116 42¼ 52½ 42½ 42 Vergara O 4 6250 84-12 JupiterTogee,RunningDhonu,Bosto 9
30Sep87-6Fpx 1 1/16 :47 1:124 1:451ft 6 116 87½ 53½ 21½ 1½ Vergara O 9 [S] 3200 85-12 Rope Tender, Patrick O.,Ryandale 10
27Sep87-13Fpx 1 1/16 :47 1:122 1:46 ft 13 116 43½ 31½ 52¾ 42¾ Higuera A R 8 6250 78-13 JohnsTomorrow,Bosto,OrientalWay 9
27Sep87—Wide
20Sep87-12Fpx 1 1/16 :474 1:132 1:452ft 21 116 86½ 75¾ 78 710 Higuera A R 8 8000 74-16 Jolly Josh, Hatamoto, Parlapiano 10
20Sep87—Wide 1/4 turn 1st time around
7Sep87-1Dmr 1 1/16 :46 1:113 1:452ft 10 116 79¼ 76 66 54¼ Vergara O 6 10000 69-14 BusinssSchool,SrosChck,NghtRomr 8
27Aug87-9Dmr 1 1/16 :454 1:112 1:441ft 34 1115 1213 1111 1010 88¾ Magallon P 8 10000 70-17 Sir Tyson, Compound,SeaAndSew 12
27Aug87—Wide 3/8 turn
17Aug87-10LA 1 1/16 :462 1:113 1:442ft 8¾ 1115 715 67 44½ 23½ Sanchez K A 6 10000 83-12 EverBrillint,RopeTendr,NightRomr 9
7Aug87-8LA 1 1/16 :462 1:114 1:434ft 2¾ 116 42 42 58½ 55¼ Vergara O 3 8000 85-13 SmellingLoope,Parlapiano,Sirluovt 7
Sep 16 SA 4f ft :50 h

S' Long Farewell

B. g. 4, by Hail and Farewell—Good Girl Friday, by Tavana
OLIVARES F 116 Br.—Brown M C (Cal) 1987 9 2 0 1 $16,700
Own.—Callahan-Coomer-Brown etal Tr.—Dorfman Leonard $10,000 1986 0 M 0 0
Lifetime 9 2 0 1 $16,700
12Oct87-2SA 1⅛ :463 1:111 1:502ft 15 118 65½ 58 69 715½ Olivares F 6 10000 61-15 OlmpcBng,Nstrdms,BlwThTrmpts 12
1Aug87-2Dmr 1 :452 1:11 1:381ft 18 117 811 55 21½ 11¼ Sibille R 3 10000 77-15 S'LongFrewell,Restg,OlimpicBingo 9
1Aug87—Bumped start
19Jly87-1Hol 1 1/16 :461 1:111 1:434ft 26 116 75¾ 53½ 34 35½ Sibille R 7 10000 84-07 ExoticArbitor,JollyJosh,S'LongFrwll 9
11Jly87-2Hol 1 :451 1:101 1:362ft 26 115 1115 911 99½ 88½ Sibille R 11 10000 72-12 Ayaabi,SrosChick,ElectricMoment 11
21Jun87-9Hol 1⅛ :464 1:11 1:492ft 9¼ 116 56 78½ 613 613½ Gryder A T 4 12500 76-14 Nostromus,Tiffni'sToy,GllntMindd 10
23May87-5Hol 1 :45 1:101 1:363ft 24 119 818 815 815 712¼ DelahoussayeE 4 32000 68-15 SumAction,UrbnCowboy,MgicLedr 8
10May87-7Hol 1 :444 1:093 1:353ft 13 115 718 717 614 413 DelhoussyeE 1 Aw24000 72-17 Recognized, Danski, Magic Leader 7
22Apr87-4Hol 1 :454 1:121 1:382ft 4¾ 122 86¾ 64 31½ 11¾ DelhoussyeE 12 M28000 71-18 SLnFrll,MAndThDrmmr,HssThGlss 12
25Mar87-4SA 6½f :214 :444 1:173ft 26 118 1010 109¾ 77½ 54¼ Olivares F 6 M45000 78-17 Stary Blue, Perg Jr.,DewanToBeat 12
Oct 22 SA 5f ft 1:024 h Oct 10 SA 4f ft :503 h Sep 30 SA 4f ft :513 h Sep 22 SA 5f ft 1:024 h

Crowning
VERGARA O 118
B. h. 6, by Raise a Native—La Mesa, by Round Table
Br.—Harbor View Farm (Ky)
Tr.—O'Mara Jon M $10,000
1987 12 1 2 1 $17,725
1986 11 0 1 0 $4,990
Turf 17 2 1 0 $29,120
Own.—McKinley D C
Lifetime 33 3 3 2 $49,485
30Oct87-2SA 1⅛ :474 1:124 1:52 gd 3½ 118 32½ 32 914 920¾ Vergara O 2 12500 48-21 OlimpicBingo,BoldSaintPt,Yippyyo 9
10Oct87-10SA 1 1/16 :48 1:121 1:44 ft 30 114 42½ 42½ 57½ 59½ Vergara O 1 22500 71-17 SiberianHero,L.A.Fire,MightyBuck 11
25Sep87-12Fpx 1 1/16 :461 1:12 1:442ft 2½ 116 42½ 31 11 13¼ Vergara O 8 c12500 89-13 Crowning,ExotcArbtor,ElctrcMmnt 9
5Sep87-9Dmr 1 1/16 :453 1:101 1:432ft 11 1095 78 86½ 1110 1111¼ Gryder A T 6 22500 72-13 Rampour, Pettrax, Passer II 11
5Sep87—Bumped start
5Aug87-9Dmr 1 1/16 :461 1:112 1:441ft 7 116 35½ 31½ 1½ 21¾ Baze R A 9 16000 77-20 Convincing,Crowning,GreyGuntlet 10
5Aug87—Bumped 1/2
4Jly87-5Hol 6½f :22 :444 1:161ft 6 116 53½ 65 54½ 43½ Santos J A 11 c20000 95-09 Stbilized,HighestScript,ShowrDcr 12
21Jun87-2Hol 6½f :221 :452 1:173ft 6½ 1115 75½ 74¾ 31½ 2¾ Sherman A B 8 16000 91-14 Bruli's Ante,Crowning,CutByGlass 10
21Jun87—Wide 3/8 turn
7Jun87-5Hol 1 :45 1:101 1:371ft 7½ 1115 21 21 22½ 34¾ Gryder A T 7 20000 72-17 Powerfull Paul, Tio Nino,Crowning 9
25May87-1Hol 6f :22 :453 1:111ft 26 116 53 65¼ 65¼ 65¼ Valenzuela P A 1 32000 82-15 MschvosMtt,MYAndQ.,FllwThDncr 7
25May87—Checked 1/2
5Apr87-7SA 1 :454 1:101 1:354ft 48 116 2hd 44 610 717¾ Douglas R R 2 50000 71-16 SiberinHro,SilvrHro,SmoothOprtor 8
5Apr87—Lost whip early drive
Sep 21 SA tr.t 4f ft :492 h Sep 15 Dmr 4f ft :491 h

Electric Moment ✻
GRYDER A T 1115
B. g. 6, by Gouscinow—Haughty Naughty, by Jean-Pierre
Br.—Cannata Mr-Mrs C (Cal)
Tr.—Wiseheart Larry $10,000
1987 14 3 2 4 $18,597
1986 14 2 3 5 $8,932
Own.—Wiseheart L
Lifetime 36 6 7 10 $31,579
15Oct87-1SA 1 1/16 :474 1:122 1:454ft 8½ 117 32 22 23 24 Kaenel J L 10 12500 68-19 TommyThoms,ElctrcMomnt,Sgmr 11
4Oct87-10Fpx 1 1/16 :462 1:123 1:442ft 31 116 78¾ 72¾ 66 67¼ Kaenel J L 6 20000 82-12 Moro Bay,BlazeFlame,Gaelic Knight 9
25Sep87-12Fpx 1 1/16 :461 1:12 1:442ft 7½ 116 2hd 2hd 21 33¼ Kaenel J L 1 12500 86-13 Crownng,ExotcArbtor,ElctrcMmnt 9
3Sep87-2Dmr 7f :223 :453 1:24 ft 5½ 118 85¼ 76¼ 67 34½ Simpson B H 2 10000 77-18 ErnKng,Pppy'sConsl,ElctrcMomnt 12
19Aug87-9Dmr 1 1/16 :453 1:111 1:432ft 23 116 32 31 22 49¾ Kaenel J L 11 16000 73-14 Dennis D., Running Debonair,Cold 11
1Aug87-2Dmr 1 :452 1:11 1:381ft 3½ 115 67½ 66 58 511 Olivares F 4 c10000 66-15 S'LongFrewell,Restg,OlimpicBingo 9
1Aug87—Bumped, pinched at start; wide into stretch
11Jly87-2Hol 1 :451 1:101 1:362ft 3½ 115 43 32½ 44 33½ Olivares F 9 10000 77-12 Ayaabi,SrosChick,ElectricMoment 11
1Jly87-2Hol 7f :222 :451 1:242ft 17 115 86 76½ 32 2no Olivares F6 10000 82-13 FblosGlc,ElctrcMmnt,DmndCtrll 11
24May87-9Hol 1⅛ :472 1:12 1:511ft 6½ 115 32½ 44 44½ 57¾ Olivares F3 10000 73-13 Nostradmus,ExoticArbitor,Disciple 9
22Mar87-10AC 1 :472 1:121 1:384m 3½ 114 49½ 56½ 42 1hd Lopez A D2 10000 79-22 ElctricMomnt,SutThrtn,DollrScholr 8
Sep 22 SA 4f ft :483 h Sep 11 Dmr 4f ft :462 h

Reserve
VALENZUELA P A 116
Dk. b. or br. h. 6, by Buckfinder—Irish Mail, by Double Jay
Br.—Keck H B (Ky)
Tr.—Hutchinson Kathy $10,000
1987 2 0 1 0 $1,100
1986 14 2 1 2 $20,162
Turf 5 0 0 0
Own.—Dolan & Roy
Lifetime 30 3 3 5 $48,437
9Oct87-6Cby 1 :481 1:123 1:381ft 2½ 116 32 41¾ 2hd 2no Warhol V L 4 12500 90-15 Sultn'sGold,Reserve,StrikeThPrinc 6
29Aug87-8Cby 6½f :22 :443 1:161ft 19 116 77¾ 710 612 612 Orona W 2 25000 88-13 Verbtim'sPride,RoleOnForli,Incens 7
26Dec86-9SA 1 1/16 :454 1:102 1:43 ft 109 116 79¼ 98¾ 1012 813½ Simpson B H 5 25000 72-13 Cold,TommyThoms,BoncngBttons 11
26Dec86—Wide into stretch
16Nov86-1Hol 1 :443 1:103 1:372ft 26 116 79 69½ 610 619½ Baze G 7 25000 56-18 Billy's Special, Slugfest, Paskanell 7
16Nov86—Wide
2Nov86-3SA 1 1/16 :461 1:103 1:412ft 28 115 611 613 616 621 Baze G 1 40000 73-10 Oricao, Idol, Tough Envoy 6
10Aug86-7Cby 1 :471 1:12 1:392ft 3½ 120 55¾ 55 22½ 22½ Kutz D 5 Aw13800 81-17 On Retainer,Reserve,AddisonSteele 6
27Jly86-10Cby 1 :47 1:113 1:373ft 5½ 119 25 43½ 44½ 34¾ Kutz D 1 35000 88-15 HollywoodHckett,Joy'sPurpos,Rsrv 5
6Jly86-7Cby 1 :47 1:122 1:384ft 10 1165 43½ 52¾ 66 63¾ Murray K C 6 Aw14300 83-15 Katzenjammer,Balaash,PatchofSun 7
25Jun86-8Cby 1 :462 1:114 1:383ft 23 121 613 612 48½ 47 Hansen R D 4 Aw14300 81-16 Siberian Hero, Balaash, Put Away 7
15Jun86-8Cby 1 1/16 Ⓣ:484 1:14 1:44 fm 19 123 106 1010 1017 1029¼ Lidberg D W 9 Aw13300 — — IlMrcolo,IronGlov,SmoothSunston 10
Nov 4 SA 4f sl :492 h ●Oct 5 Cby 4f ft :482 h Sep 30 Cby 3f ft :351 h Sep 22 Cby 4f ft :481 h

Laurel's Time
PATTERSON A 116
Dk. b. or br. g. 5, by Olden Times—Laurel Lark, by T V Lark
Br.—Whitney T P (NY)
Tr.—Baker James R $10,000
1987 6 0 2 0 $6,300
1986 10 1 1 2 $13,857
Turf 1 0 0 0
Own.—Baker J R
Lifetime 21 1 3 3 $22,757
24Oct87-1SA 6f :212 :45 1:103gd 24 116 57 78¾ 34 21¾ Patterson A1 10000 83-17 Cool'nScndlos,Lrl'sTm,HvrngPrsnc 9
17Oct87-1SA 7f :224 :46 1:241ft 44 114 31½ 43 46½ 55½ Patterson A5 10500 73-16 InspirdToo,ErniKing,HovrngPrsnc 10
20Sep87-12Fpx 1 1/16 :474 1:132 1:452ft 6 116 64 64½ 65½ 57 Patterson A7 8000 77-16 Jolly Josh, Halamoto, Parlapiano 10
20Sep87—Wide
27Aug87-9Dmr 1 1/16 :454 1:112 1:441ft 50 116 65¼ 1½ 11½ 44¼ Patterson A11 10000 74-17 Sir Tyson, Compound,SeaAndSew 12
8Aug87-11LA 1 1/16 :45 1:111 1:434ft 10 116 22½ 42½ 78 86½ Patterson A8 12500 83-13 ExoticArbitor,Dncebl,DickAndHugh 9
25Jly87-1Hol 6f :224 :462 1:12 ft 16 115 2½ 21½ 22½ 24 Patterson A6 10000 79-16 Numpkins, Laurel's Time,Valcreon 10
20Aug86-9Dmr 1 1/16 :453 1:102 1:421ft 26 116 53½ 74 811 814¼ Douglas R R3 16000 75-11 OlimpicBingo,RedDusty,Halamoto 10
20Aug86—Wide into stretch
6Aug86-5Dmr 1⅛ Ⓣ:482 1:124 1:502fm 118 117 86¾ 109¼ 1016 1017¼ Douglas R R8 Aw20000 65-14 FlyingSnow,Nurely,CashInTheBnk 10
28Jun86-9Hol 1⅛ :46 1:104 1:494ft 10 116 44½ 45½ 32 35½ Solis A3 20000 82-12 CertinTret,MrkInTheSky,Lurl'sTim 7
8Jun86-9Hol 1 :46 1:11 1:364ft 15 116 54½ 75¾ 44 53 Solis A6 20000 76-11 Kunto, OlimpicBingo,DoubleDeficit 9
8Jun86—Wide 3/8 turn
Oct 5 SA 4f ft :491 h

Come On Rain
~~**NO RIDER**~~ Castanon 113
B. g. 3, by Today 'n Tomorrow—Terratina, by Terresto
Br.—Harmony Farms (Cal)
Tr.—Davis Mark $10,000
1987 12 1 0 0 $3,538
1986 3 M 0 0
Own.—Davis M
Lifetime 15 1 0 0 $3,538
25Oct87-2SA 6f :22 :45 1:103gd 60 115 1112 1113 1114 1117¼ Vergara O 10 10000 68-19 CourgeRuler,John'sJove,JulioNMe 11
15Oct87-11Fno 6f :22 :45 1:091ft 7 115 33 46½ 49 412½ Brinkerhoff D 5 12500 81-15 Page Mr. Glory, Elf King,SierraDan 6
7Oct87-3Fno 6f :213 :444 1:10 ft 4¾ 115 86¾ 67 44 12 BrinkrhoffD 6 ⓈM12500 90-11 ComeOnRin,CndinGusto,‡Dr. Crroll 10
26Sep87-7Fpx 1 1/16 :464 1:122 1:45 ft 41 1095 73¾ 88 714 718¼ Sanchez K A 5 10500 68-11 Jan'sHatTrick,DareToBeMore,Clmo 9
19Sep87-4Fpx 1 1/16 :471 1:133 1:47 ft 41 1055 63 65 76½ 610 Sanchez K A 4 8500 66-18 WhtShowrs,JohnsTomorrw,RylBlrr 9
20Aug87-4LA 1 1/16 :463 1:122 1:451ft 5¾ 115 42½ 32½ 32¼ 45½ Patterson A 8 M12500 77-07 ClrenceHouse,Premeditted,IcStorm 9
13Aug87-2LA 1 1/16 :453 1:121 1:461ft 10 115 46½ 43 33 42¾ Patterson A 1 M12500 75-12 GilddCjun,CloudyTrip,Nwl'sFrstSon 8
19Apr87-4SA 6f :214 :45 1:102ft 97 116 109¼ 1012 912 914¼ Gomez R5 M45000 72-17 AtTheRitz,Guggen,PolynesinChief 10
1Apr87-6SA 1 :463 1:112 1:38 ft 75 115 915 915 716 620¼ Gomez R8 ⓈM28000 58-23 PeteNewell,HssTheGlss,‡ProprTop 10
1Apr87—Off slowly; wide
18Mar87-2SA 1 1/16 :463 1:121 1:461ft 149 116 78½ 1011 817 815¾ Gomez R11 M28000 54-17 TrnBckJohn,MmBond,StlltExprss 12
●Sep 12 Fpx 5f ft 1:011 h

when the 17-1 longest shot in the field defeated the 15-1 second-longest shot to surprise. The fans booed lustily when the number came back to pay only $444.50 for $5, but that's what you get sometimes when you back two longshots in the exacta—a ridiculous underlay.

The eighth race presented Quinn with a dilemma. He loved Ferdinand, but he was afraid that since this was merely a prep for the $3 million Breeders Cup Classic two weeks hence (which Ferdinand would win), the horse might not be asked for his top performance, especially since the track was a bit muddy. The 8-5 price looked like stealing, but only if Ferdinand would be going full out. Quinn decided to pass. Ferdinand won easily.

It was now the final race of the day and Quinn had mostly sat on his hands after scoring heavily in the first two races—not because of some fear of losing his profits, but because very little had turned up that interested him. He did like the last race, however. In post position order, here was his complete line, and the crowd's, for the final race:

	Q	C
#1 Reason To Study	3-1	7-2
#2 Fabulous Gaelic	4-1	5-1
#3 Majestuso	15-1	5-1
#4 Rope Tender	3-1	14-1
#5 S' Long Farewell	–	17-1
#6 Crowning	25-1	16-1
#7 Electric Moment	7-1	7-2
#8 Reserve	30-1	6-1
#9 Laurel's Time	25-1	7-1
#10 Come On Rain	–	50-1

Quinn salivated over the price on Rope Tender. Since leaving Del Mar as a dull longshot, the horse had perked up while beating up on cheaper horses. However, since $10,000 was the bottom of the Santa Anita claiming barrel, he wasn't exactly stepping up to face Secretariat today. And, at 14-1, Rope Tender was certainly worth a play if you gave him any shot at all.

The required payoffs for the $5 exacta are reproduced in the upper part of the squares on page 139, with the prices that met the cutoff left in.

Note that there were 10 possible plays, which means we had to subtract 9 losing bets multiplied by $5 per play, or $45 per combination. That knocked out 1-2, 2-1, and 4-9. It's a cheerless world at times, for

	1³	2⁴	3¹⁵	4³	5⁻	6²⁵	7⁷	8³⁰	9²⁵	10⁻
1³	X	(141) ¹¹⁰		(278) ⁵⁵						
2⁴	(152) ¹¹⁹	X		(483) ¹¹⁸						
3				X						
4³	(377) ⁵⁸	(574) ¹¹⁰	(477) ¹⁵⁵	X		(1056) ⁵⁸³	(262) ¹⁷⁵		(62) ⁵⁸³	

Reason To Study outnodded Fabulous Gaelic with the 1-2 exacta returning $141.00. Rope Tender finished sixth.

Despite the loss in the nightcap, Quinn had enjoyed an excellent day by sticking with his overlays. He was concerned not just with his top picks, but with getting fair value for his plays. Whenever he had a questionable race, he passed.

Make a line for every race that interests you. Check all the pools. Play only when the crowd offers you enough value.

And if you find enough discrepancies between your opinion and the crowd's—and if you're right enough of the time—you can become a successful player at the racetrack.

A $100,000 SCORE

Yes, the check on the cover of this book is real. February 3, 1990 will long remain an important part of racing history for me. No, not because it was the date of Willie Shoemaker's last career ride. I'll remember the day because I hit a pick 6 that was worth $114,446.40, using the strategy outlined in this book.

The pot began to build on Thursday, two days before, when February opened with no one hitting all six winners at Santa Anita. The pick 6 pool was a mere $156,570 so the carryover was $62,565.

I went over Friday's card, intending to play a pick 6, but the day looked very tough. I figured that my chance of hitting all six was too slim for the sheet I would have played, so I passed. Good choice. The pool was $253,901 and again no one hit, which set up the big day Saturday.

The pick 6 pool for Saturday figured to be gigantic. First, there was the now two-day carryover of $164,024. Second, even casual fans would be drawn to the track and to the satellites for Shoemaker's farewell.

And I liked the card.

Since this isn't a book about handicapping, I won't go into all the factors and angles that made me choose the horses I did. Suffice it to say that none of them was impossible. The key, as it always seems to be when a big ticket comes down, was making out the best ticket for the least money.

My total investment was $912, spread over four tickets. The actual winning ticket appears below.

When I first begin to make out a pick 6, I start by listing every horse I think can reasonably win. It would be nice to use one giant ticket to cover all these horses—though even if these contenders win 80% of their respective races I would win the pick 6 only 26% of the time—but such a giant ticket often would cost five figures. I usually play between $500 and $1500 on a pick 6, so I try to keep my ticket within these boundaries.

In the case of the big one, my original non-throwouts were 4 x 3 x 2 x 8 x 6 x 5. This would cost $11,520. So now it was time to handicap seriously.

I opened with my four horses in the second race, the start of the pick 6. It was a maiden race, so I looked for lightly raced horses who had shown speed and for live first-time starters. Max The Baker (7) and Norths Time (3) had both run well previously and the latter was adding lasix. They would both have to be used. There were two unknowns with positive angles—Itsthefax (4) was shipping in from Caliente off a four-month layoff for a trainer who does exceptionally well with shippers and layoff horses. The other was Akrokerami (5) who was a first-timer from the exceedingly hot David Hofmans barn. Both these trainers seem to do much better when their mystery horses get tote action—so I decided to definitely use 7 and 3, and if both the unknowns got good tote action I would use them both; if either or both were dead on the board the corpse would be eliminated.

Two horses looked far above the others in the third race—Ron Bon (4) and Frost Free (5). I gave a third horse (Pinecutter, 6) a small chance. But I quickly decided that Pinecutter could win only if both the top two horses ran dull races, so I zapped Pinecutter. I couldn't separate my two choices, and neither would the crowd as Ron Bon would go off at 9-5 and Frost Free at 2-1.

The fourth took only a short time to handicap as again two horses stood out—TV Lord (5) and Sam McGee (6). TV Lord had just blitzed a maiden field while Sam McGee had just won a claiming race in excellent time. TV Lord went off at 6-5 and Sam McGee at 9-5.

The fifth looked like my first race to take a shot. It was the Shoemaker farewell race so he had been permitted to choose any mount in the field.

I decided to make his selection, Patchy Groundfog (1), one of my keys. However, the race looked wide open and I eventually used five of my other seven contenders—Exemplary Leader (3), Nediym (6), Colson (8), Oraibi (9) and Bosphorus (11). Shoemaker figured to be way overbet so I would get decent value if he lost; if he won, I'd be alive to four horses in the sixth race.

While I originally considered six horses in the sixth race, I eventually narrowed my contenders to four—Pleasure Bought (2), Caseys Romance (7), Just Say Whoa (6), and Via May (8). However, I liked two of these (Pleasure Bought and Caseys Romance) better than the other two. My saver ticket if Patchy Groundfog lost was going to cost $1280 which would bring the total to more than I could afford, so I made the day's key decision—I decided that if Patchy Groundfog lost, I would go solely with Pleasure Bought, who figured to enjoy the seven-furlong distance. This would save me $640 and make the ticket playable.

The seventh and final leg was a grass race in which only two of the eight entrants had previously competed locally on the turf. I knew I had to spread. I used the favorite (Sandskipper, 7) who had raced on the lawn before along with two horses well-bred for the green (Fraulein Maria, 4 and Miss Malibu, 6) with one mystery Argentine shipper (Riches, 2). I also used a small saver with Basic Star (8) which would be alive only if Patchy Groundfog won the fifth.

Before deciding on the final ticket, I watched the betting in the second race. Sure enough, Itsthefax, who had been 5-2 in the morning line, was getting no action whatsoever. I bounced him, thereby cutting my costs by 25%. I left in the first-timer Akrokerami, who was getting pounded on the board.

I wound up sending through just four tickets, a virtual breeze since often I fill out as many as 60 or 70 cards with various combinations of A's, B's, C's, savers, this-must-win or that's-alive-only-with-the-other.

Norths Time ($9.80) held off the late threat by Max The Baker to win the second.
Frost Free ($6.80) and Ron Bon ran 1-2 in the third.
Sam McGee ($5.60) and TV Lord ran 1-2 in the fourth.
Exemplary Leader ($26.80) paid much bigger than he should have since people wanted souvenirs of the Shoe's last ride and banged Patchy Groundfog to a ridiculous 3-5 in the fifth.
Pleasure Bought ($7.20), a single since Patchy Groundfog had been

beaten, came from seventh at the half to win the sixth going away.

Fraulein Maria ($23.60) impressed in her first turf start to take the seventh.

Only four people had the pick 6, which returned a sweet $114,464.40. I also collected 12 of those fancy $1920 fives, which brought the whole kitty to $137,486.40. Even after the 20% takeout, that left Santa Anita to pay me a pleasant $109,989.40.

Sometimes this stuff does work.

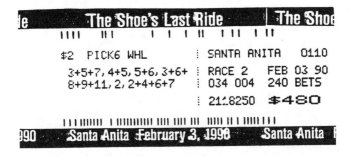

FOURTH RACE
Santa Anita
FEBRUARY 3, 1990

6 FURLONGS. (1.07⅘) ALLOWANCE. Purse $34,000. 4-year-olds and upward which are non-winners of $3,000 other than maiden or claiming. Weights, 4-year-olds, 120 lbs.; older, 121 lbs. Non-winners of a race other than claiming allowed 3 lbs.

Value of race $34,000; value to winner $18,700; second $6,800; third $5,100; fourth $2,550; fifth $850. Mutuel pool $1,122,408.

Last Raced	Horse	Eqt	A	Wt	PP	St	¼	½	Str	Fin	Jockey	Odds $1
21Jan90 5SA1	Sam McGee		5	118	6	2	21½	2½	11½	12½	Valenzuela P A	1.80
5Jan90 6SA1	T. V. Lord		4	120	5	5	4½	31½	24	25½	Pedroza M A	1.30
8Jun89 2Hol1	Chestnut Freeze		6	113	2	6	6	6	51½	32½	Nakatani C S5	12.10
5Jan90 7SA8	Tuffact Too		4	120	3	4	31½	41½	4hd	43½	Stevens G L	6.60
21Apr89 3SA5	Pieds Promise		4	120	1	1	51½	5hd	6	54½	Davis R G	22.40
31Dec89 3SA5	Ole Hank McGill	b	4	120	4	3	1hd	1hd	31	6	Baze R A	5.70

OFF AT 2:08. Start good. Won driving. Time, :21⅘, :45⅗, :57⅘, 1:10⅗ Track fast.

$2 Mutuel Prices:

6-SAM MCGEE	5.60	3.20	2.60
5-T. V. LORD		2.80	2.40
2-CHESTNUT FREEZE			2.80

Ch. g, by It's Freezing—Try Azimycin, by Cleo. Trainer Shulman Sanford. Bred by Wrenn B-G-Ruby (Ky).

FIFTH RACE
Santa Anita
FEBRUARY 3, 1990

1 MILE.(Turf). (1.32⅗) LEGEND'S LAST RIDE HANDICAP. $100,000 added. 4-year-olds and upward. By subscription of $50 each to accompany the nomination, $250 to pass the entry box, $250 additional to start, with $100,000 added, of which $20,000 to second, $15,000 to third, $7,500 to fourth and $2,500 to fifth. Weights, Tuesday, January 30. Highweights preferred. Starters to be named through the entry box by the closing time of entries. A trophy will be presented to the owner of the winner. This race will be Bill Shoemaker's final ride. In the event that his mount is withdrawn prior to the running of the race, any one of the remaining entrants' jockeys will be subject to replacement by Bill Shoemaker. The undersigned agrees to the aforementioned conditions that the undersigned's horse may be ridden by Bill Shoemaker. Closed Friday, January 26, 1990 with 42 nominations.

Value of race $107,850; value to winner $62,850; second $20,000; third $15,000; fourth $7,500; fifth $2,500. Mutuel pool $1,009,882. Exacta Pool $1,175,504.

Last Raced	Horse	Eqt	A	Wt	PP	St	¼	½	¾	Str	Fin	Jockey	Odds $1
26Dec89 8SA2	Exemplary Leader		4	116	2	8	7hd	9½	91	5hd	1½	Delahoussaye E	12.40
13Jan90 8BM	Happy Toss		5	116	1	5	3hd	3hd	4½	3hd	2½	Toro F	23.50
13Jan90 8SA2	Oraibi		5	117	9	2	41	41	31	41	3hd	Black C A	16.00
31Dec89 8SA2	Patchy Groundfog		7	118	8	3	21	21	21	21	4½	Shoemaker W	.70
12Jan90 8SA4	Shining Steel		4	115	4	4	51	6hd	5½	61½	5nk	Davis R G	38.20
14Jan90 8SA8	River Master		4	116	6	6	81½	71	7½	71	6nk	Hawley S	26.70
20Jan90 3SA3	Bosphorus		5	115	11	7	11	8hd	81½	8½	71½	McCarron C J	12.40
16Dec89 7BM3	Nediym		5	115	5	9	9hd	10½	101½	91½	8no	Baze R A	5.70
4Jan90 8SA1	Splendor Catch		6	116	3	1	1½	1½	1hd	1hd	91½	Stevens G L	22.40
21Jan90 3SA3	Rampoldi		4	115	10	11	101	11	11	10hd	101½	Boulanger G	28.80
22Oct89 5Fra1	Colson		4	116	7	10	61	5½	6hd	11	11	Valenzuela P A	13.90

OFF AT 2:47. Start good. Won driving. Time, :22⅘, :46, 1:10, 1:21⅘, 1:34⅗ Course firm.

$2 Mutuel Prices:

3-EXEMPLARY LEADER	26.80	11.20	7.00
2-HAPPY TOSS		20.20	13.60
9-ORAIBI			8.20

$5 EXACTA 3-2 PAID $922.00.

Dk. b. or br. c, by Vigors—Paradigmatic, by Aristocratic. Trainer Mayberry Brian A. Bred by Kenwood Stable II (Ky).

SIXTH RACE
Santa Anita
FEBRUARY 3, 1990

7 FURLONGS. (1.20) MAIDEN. Purse $30,000. Fillies. 3-year-olds. Weight, 117 lbs. (Non-starters for a claiming price of $32,000 or less in their last three starts preferred).

Value of race $30,000; value to winner $16,500; second $6,000; third $4,500; fourth $2,250; fifth $750. Mutuel pool $881,458.

Last Raced	Horse	Eqt	A	Wt	PP	St	¼	½	Str	Fin	Jockey	Odds $1
13Jan90 4SA2	Pleasure Bought	b	3	117	2	7	7hd	72	42	12½	Baze R A	2.60
6Jan90 4SA6	Classic Ice		3	117	5	3	4hd	31	2½	22½	Solis A	15.30
10Dec89 4Hol5	Lucky Kate		3	117	4	5	52½	2½	1hd	31	Valenzuela P A	8.00
13Jan90 4SA3	Just Say Whoa		3	112	6	6	6½	6hd	6hd	4½	Nakatani C S5	6.10
21Jan90 4SA6	Sunday Best		3	117	1	8	8	8	8	52½	Black C A	73.60
21Jan90 4SA2	Via May	b	3	117	8	1	2½	4hd	5hd	6½	Davis R G	6.30
6Jan90 4SA3	Casey's Romance		3	117	7	2	1hd	51	72	7½	Delahoussaye E	2.30
10Dec89 4Hol4	War Commandress		3	117	3	4	3hd	1hd	31	8	McCarron C J	5.60

OFF AT 3:23. Start good. Won driving. Time, :22⅗, :45⅘, 1:12⅘, 1:25⅗ Track fast.

$2 Mutuel Prices:

2-PLEASURE BOUGHT	7.20	4.20	3.60
5-CLASSIC ICE		12.40	7.40
4-LUCKY KATE			6.60

Dk. b. or br. f, (Apr), by Marfa—Oversold, by Barbizon. Trainer Palma Hector O. Bred by Bettersworth J R (Ky).

SEVENTH RACE
Santa Anita
FEBRUARY 3, 1990

1 MILE.(Turf). (1.32⅗) ALLOWANCE. Purse $37,000. Fillies and mares. 4-year-olds and upward, which are non-winners of $3,000 other than maiden, claiming or starter races. Weights, 4-year-olds 119 lbs.; older 120 lbs. Non-winners of a race other than claiming at one mile or over, allowed 2 lbs. (winners that have started for a claiming of $25,000 or less in their last 3 starts, and maidens that are non-starters for a claiming price have 2nd preference.

Value of race $37,000; value to winner $20,350; second $7,400; third $5,550; fourth $2,775; fifth $925. Mutuel pool $633,364. Exacta pool $790,806.

Last Raced	Horse	Eqt	A	Wt	PP	St	¼	½	¾	Str	Fin	Jockey	Odds $1
12Jan90 7SA8	Fraulein Maria		4	117	4	2	6hd	61	3hd	2hd	11½	Stevens G L	10.80
8Nov89 6Arg3	Riches		4	119	2	7	8	8	73	43	2½	Delahoussaye E	5.10
27Jan90 6SA9	Yankee Hostess		4	112	5	4	22	21½	1hd	1½	32	Nakatani C S5	30.40
14Jan90 1SA1	Free Living	b	4	117	1	1	1hd	1hd	21	31½	4hd	Sibille R	9.60
6Jan90 3SA8	Sandskipper		5	120	7	8	77	75	51	5½	52½	Toro F	2.00
19Jan90 5SA3	Miss Malibu		4	112	6	5	4hd	4hd	6hd	62	64	Jauregui L H5	4.80
31Dec89 4SA1	Lovlier Laura	b	4	119	3	3	52½	3½	41	70	711	McCarron C J	4.50
24Jan90 8SA8	Basic Star		5	120	8	6	3hd	5½	8	8	8	Baze R A	6.30

OFF AT 3:54. Start good. Won driving. Time, :22⅘, :46, 1:10⅘, 1:22⅘, 1:35⅗ Course firm.

$2 Mutuel Prices:

4-FRAULEIN MARIA	23.60	9.20	7.20
2-RICHES		6.20	5.40
5-YANKEE HOSTESS			9.60

$5 EXACTA 4-2 PAID $374.50.

B. f, by Darby Creek Road—Washoe Zephyr, by Windy Sea. Trainer Young Steven W. Bred by Lerille A J (Cal).

$2 Pick Six (3-5-6-3-2-4) Paid $114,446.40 for 6 Wins Including $164,024.22 Carry-over Pool; 4 Tickets. 5 Wins Paid $1,920.00; 153 Tickets. Pool $735,140.

AFTERWORD

I wrote the first edition of this book in 1988. Over the years, players have asked me if there's going to be a revised version, an update for the 21st century. I've told them that as long as $2 + 2 = 4$, the mathematics of gambling are never going to change. The 1988 version will still work in 2088.

You still have to shop for value. And if you're right often enough, you can win, if you have the discipline to play only when you're getting the best of it.

But the types of bets available have changed, and so will the opportunities for players. It's not unusual for a track to offer rolling daily doubles, so you can bet the double not only on races 1-2 but on 5-6 and 6-7 as well. Somewhere, you can find a place pick all, a double quinella, a pick 5, a futures bet, and a twin trifecta. Racebooks will continue to offer proposition and matchup bets.

New to the scene in recent years has been the guaranteed pool, generally a pick 6 in which the track guarantees the pool to be a certain size and will make up the difference if there's a betting shortfall. These have turned out to be mostly worthless, since players bet more than the guarantee so there's no edge; however, occasionally they have turned out to be windfalls, such as when Hawthorne offered a $100,000 guarantee and considerably less than that was bet.

These days, more than 80% of the money bet at most tracks comes in from somewhere other than the facility. Players can bet over the phone, at an off-track parlor, at a nearby simulcast center, over the Internet, at an Indian reservation—the places to play keep expanding. And there's the presence of the offshore racebooks, which keep chugging away despite the occasional scandalous disappearance or bankruptcy which leaves players with a total loss.

Despite the best efforts of legislators and the racing industry to mess things up (you often need two or more accounts to play the tracks you want, and many places bar players from certain states from betting on racing in certain other states), this off-course growth is likely to continue. Players want convenience. No longer do they want to drive an hour to place a bet, nor do they want to be restricted to their own local $2,500 claimers. They want to be able to watch races from everywhere and bet everywhere with as few obstacles as possible.

Players have also come to realize that with takeouts creeping ever higher— not a single state currently offers an exacta takeout of less than 19%, and trifecta takeouts of 25% or more are commonplace—to stay in the game they are demanding rebates. Many tracks offer a players club in which players hand a card to a teller when they bet, to qualify for small (generally less than 1%) rebates which may be given in cash or merchandise or discounted admissions.

But major rebate centers have emerged, changing the face of the game for big players. These shops, located far from racetracks but with contracts that enable them to send their bets into track pools, have become the betting parlor of choice for many of the country's largest bettors. Though their contracts expressly forbid such rebates, these shops continue to exist in a speakeasy world where players must be recommended to get in, bettors must often wager a required minimum amount to stay in, and no paperwork divulges any rebate information. These shops offer varying rebates depending on their contract with a particular track, but it's not unheard of for some players to get back more than 12% on certain bets at certain tracks. If he bets high enough, a break-even player who averages a 6% rebate can make a nice living. A guy who loses 4% but gets back 10% will do equally as well.

These rebate shops have made a huge impact on the toteboard. Generous rebates have encouraged big players to become even bigger players. Many of them wager at the last minute, their giant bets not being recorded on the track toteboards until the race is half over. As a result, it's not uncommon for players to bet a horse who's 3-1 with thirty seconds to post, only to learn he actually went off at 9-5.

That means that it's not always possible to predict the final odds with the accuracy of bygone days. Certainly there still are ways to do so, but it takes some doing. For instance, you can calculate what the horse is paying in the daily double and in the exacta, so that if he's 4-1 in both those pools but 6-1 in the win pool late in the betting, it's reasonable to assume that his odds will come down. Although you can do this in your head, some players use calculators or computer programs to figure this.

One thing that hasn't changed, and probably never will, is that misguided and dishonest vendors will continue to hawk money-management schemes that attempt to turn losses into profits. You can, in fact, easily come up with some group of results in which Big Al's Secret Plan would have outperformed Kelly betting or flat betting. Or where some parlay method would have turned a small profit into a large one.

But the truth is this: Your long-range expectation is *exactly* the same as your single-bet expectation. In other words, if a certain method loses 15% on average, it will lose 15% long-term *no matter how the bets are manipulated*. Whether you raise your bets after a win or after a loss, whether you wait for some pattern to show itself, whether you play a constant percentage of your bankroll—it doesn't matter in the long run. The mathematical truths behind this statement can be found in many books, including those by Allan Wilson (*The Casino Gambler's Guide*) and Edward Thorpe (*The Mathematics Of Gambling*).

What counts is your ability to perceive the *true odds* of an event, then take advantage when there's a discrepancy between your perception and the crowd's odds. This is easier said than done, but it *can* be done. More than ever, the crowd pounds the obvious figure horses into unprofitability. Favorites, which at the time of the first printing of this book were shown to have lost half the track take, now lose just about the take; a survey of 200,000 favorites in the January 2000 edition of *Meadow's Racing Monthly* showed that betting every favorite now loses 19%.

There remains a place for money management at the racetrack. A very important place. Maybe even more important than being able to handicap (though let's not minimize that, either).

To take a ridiculous example, let's say a player hits 99% winners but bets his entire bankroll on every race. As soon as he hits a loser, he's broke. The reason—bad money management, not bad handicapping.

Knowing your acceptable odds for a particular bet, and then playing only when you get those odds, should remain your guiding principle. Let the crowd focus on picking winners. You should be focusing on shopping for value.

Most of the time, we're going to be wrong about a race. When we are right, we should get rewarded.

Money management alone won't turn a losing player into a winner. It takes hard work to win, and even hard work is no guarantee of success at the racetrack. Due to the takeout, most players must lose. But that doesn't mean *you* have to lose. Do the work and stay disciplined in the betting arena, and you just might be among that select group of individuals who can honestly say, "I beat the races."

—Barry Meadow
July 2002

MORE GREAT STUFF FROM BARRY MEADOW

Blackjack Autumn: A True Tale of Life, Death, and Splitting Tens in Winnemucca. What is it like to take two months from your life to play blackjack in every casino in Nevada? The author set out alone with one suitcase, one tape recorder, and $8,000 on the gambling adventure of a lifetime. This wise, witty true tale takes you deep into a little-known world in a book the Las Vegas Review-Journal called "hilarious, enlightening, and suspenseful."

Players Guide To Nevada Racebooks. This 100-booklet is the definitive guide to the Nevada racebook scene. The author visited every racebook in the state to discover everything you need to know about betting in a casino racebook. You'll learn how to qualify for free rooms and meals, where to get free Daily Racing Forms, who offers individual TV monitors at your seat, and survival tips for making the most money during your playing time.

Professional Harness Betting. This 300-page manual is must reading for anyone who wants to win substantial money at the harness races. Easy to understand and simple to use, this book will give you the skills you need to become a winning player. Handicapping harness racing is completely different from thoroughbred racing, and this step-by-step instructional guide will show you how to succeed. The book comes with a one-hour audio tape.

Secrets Of The Pick 6. Have you ever wondered how to hit those six-figure payoffs which can change your life? This 43-page booklet covers everything you need to know about playing the Pick 6, with further details that we didn't have space for in the book you're currently reading. How big should you bet? How can you calculate your typical Pick 6 payoff for a particular ticket? When should you pass the Pick 6, even with a carryover?

Meadow's Racing Monthly. This hard-hitting, award-winning newsletter covers every aspect of handicapping and money management. We give you the latest ideas about how to beat the races, test systems on a large database, and provide the kind of statistical analysis of handicapping ideas that are available nowhere else, along with exclusive investigative articles. Everything we do is designed to help you make money or save money at the track.

Master Win Ratings. This daily handicapping service provides ratings, on a scale of 1 to 35, for every horse that races in California. Call our toll-free phone lines or get the ratings delivered by e-mail to quickly determine the top choices and contenders. In a survey of 15 services by SportStat, only Master Win Ratings finished in the top 3 in win, place, show, and ROI percentages. This is not a selection service, but an excellent aid to your own handicapping.

Audiotapes ($15 each) may be ordered separately for:
Money Secrets At The Racetrack
Professional Harness Betting
Master Win Ratings

For further information, go to *www.trpublishing.com* or call (800) 378-2211

ABOUT THE AUTHOR

Barry Meadow has spent more than 30 years in the gambling world and has written for many publications on a wide variety of gambling topics.

Currently he produces *Meadow's Racing Monthly*, a handicapping and money-management newsletter, and *Master Win Ratings*, a handicapping service for thoroughbreds.

He lives in California.